Anne Kernaleguen   Clothing Designs for the Handicapped

D1717251

The University
of Alberta Press
1978

First published by
The University of Alberta Press
Edmonton, Alberta, Canada
1978

Copyright © 1978 The University of Alberta Press

Canadian Cataloguing in Publication Data

Kernaleguen, Anne, 1926–
  Clothing designs for the handicapped

  Bibliography: p.
  ISBN 0-88864-020-X

  1. Handicapped—Clothing. I. Title.
  TT648.K47   646.47   C78-002002-2

Book design by Peter Bartl

Printed by Hignell Printing Ltd.,
Winnipeg, Manitoba, Canada

to my natural and
adoptive parents

Acknowledgments

Appreciation is expressed to all who have contributed to the research project which made this publication possible.

To the handicapped themselves, their families and those in charge of their care, for offering comments, making suggestions, and reacting to various clothing items.

To funding agencies for their support:
The Government of Alberta
Medical Services Research Foundation
  of Alberta
U. of A. Alumni—Alma Mater Fund
U. of A. President's N.R.C. Fund

To the undergraduate and graduate students and staff who contributed to the project, namely: Jean Nielsen, Patricia Moore Juzwishin, Joyce Brett, Sheila McNaughtan, Heather MacDonald, Christine Feniak, Norma Jean Heine, Elva Nilsen, Susan Horvath, and Hilary Fedoruk.

To the Canadian Red Cross, Metric Commission, Multiple Sclerosis Association, Women's Division of the Red Deer Exhibition and other organizations which offered help and encouragement.

To Laurie Sims for photography, and to Peter Bartl, Associate Professor of Art and Design, for the design and layout of this publication.

To Terry Garrett for typing assistance.

Contents

Introduction

Introduction

Since chronic illness may be a slow insidious process with mild beginnings or may be caused by a sudden or acute illness, accurate statistics as to the number of individuals afflicted are not readily available. Due mainly to disabling diseases, traffic and industrial accidents, and longer life expectancy, there is a growing population of handicapped in our society today. This increases the likelihood that individual families will have to cope with the temporary or permanent disablement of one of their members during some stage of the life cycle. As well, the possibility that more and more handicapped individuals will become the responsibility of auxiliary hospitals and senior citizen homes appears inevitable.

As well as increasing in number, the handicapped are becoming more visible. More educational and occupational opportunities are open to them than ever before. There is a growing realization that a physical disability does not prevent an individual from being socially functional and economically productive. Despite these trends, there has been and continues to be, a serious neglect by society in the area of developing adequate resources to aid disabled persons in coping with their disrupted capability to carry out the simple but basic tasks related to everyday living.

Rehabilitation has been referred to as an integral part of clinical, non-institutional, and community responsibility in meeting the problems of the disabled. Implicit in the many definitions of the term rehabilitation is the concept that it is a responsibility of society, requiring a team approach, to help the temporarily or permanently handicapped make use of their capacities for developing their latent potential for self respect, independence, usefulness, hope, and happiness. Most of all, rehabilitation is an optimistic process geared to improving the quality of life for all society.

The significance of clothing to the total rehabilitation of the physically disabled person merits study. Clothing is not a trivial aspect of our daily lives. It is essential to physical, social, and psychological well-being. Physically, clothing specially designed for the disabled person allows independence in dressing and fulfils altered needs of comfort and safety. The satisfaction gained from independence in dressing as well as the pride and enhanced self-esteem that comes from looking attractive, and in turn, the favorable reactions which that attractiveness elicits from others, are conducive to psychological well-being. In addition, the kind of clothing which meets functional requirements, yet conforms in appearance to peer group standards and fashion trends, contributes to the social adjustment of the physically disabled person.

Any deviation from the norm which renders success more difficult may be considered a handicap. A physical deviation in height and weight, for example, may be a handicap for some members of society but not for others. Whether or not such a deviation becomes a handicap depends on one's perception of it. Hence, a disabling condition is not always a handicap and many able-bodied persons suffer from handicaps perceivable only to themselves, while many disabled people are coping so well that their condition poses no handicap to them.

Every human being, handicapped or not, is unique. It follows that each person has different needs, wants, likes, and dislikes. The clothing modifications which will prove helpful to one person may not be so for another. The author has endeavored to present many solutions to common problems, fully cognizant of the fact that all solutions will not be equally good for everyone. By presenting a multitude of ideas, it is hoped that all those seeking help may be able to find some suggestions that would enable them to cope with their specific clothing problems.

Basic to this book is the author's conviction that clothing for everyone should be comfortable, attractive, fashionable, and easy to put on and take off. In other words, the type of clothing worn should enable the individual to be a happier, more productive member of society. Since the handicapped may have different and specific needs, clothing designed to meet these needs can easily become "special clothing" which emphasizes, rather than minimizes, a handicap. Clothing for the handicapped should be regular clothing with added inconspicuous features or modifications designed to maximize the personal satisfaction of the wearer by accommodating his individual needs.

Research and information concerning specially designed clothing for the physically disabled has been scattered and fragmentary. Several theses have been directed to this problem, but due to the resources required to test the feasibility of certain design solutions, only limited sample sizes have been used. No follow-up research has been documented in these cases. Of particular significance in a number of studies is the substantial psychological benefit which more comfortable clothing imparted to the few who were involved.

Commercial production and distribution of specially designed clothing has also been attempted. Many problems are encountered in such projects. Not only are they dependent on a limited market for success, but the minority group which constitutes that market possesses extreme individual variations and needs. The result of these interacting factors is a restricted range of choice and a much higher cost per item than that of goods produced for the mass market.

This publication of easy-to-follow directions for alterations to ready-to-wear for people with special needs should be of particular value to those professionals in counselling and helping positions such as occupational therapists and physiotherapists, public health nurses, social workers, clothing designers, and design students. It is also hoped that it will be valuable to community workers in their endeavors to help the families of handicapped individuals or the disabled themselves. This publication is geared to the average home sewer who can follow directions and operate a sewing machine. The liberal use of illustrations should make the instructions that much easier to comprehend.

General information on clothing for special groups

The term "Clothing for the Handicapped" is defined as clothing for anyone who temporarily or permanently has special clothing needs. It is intended to provide the following, in order of priority:

Independence in that the individual will be able to take care of his own personal needs as much as possible.

Appearance comparable to that of others with whom he interacts in his everyday activities, in that the wearer will be dressed in clothing which is currently popular in style and does not single out the wearer in any way.

Concealment of the handicap as much as possible or at least no attraction of attention to it.

Physical comfort in that such clothing will not restrict physical movement nor cause undue pain, and will help maintain proper body temperature.

Psychological comfort in that such clothing will contribute to a sense of well-being for the wearer.

Safety in that it will not present undue accident hazards.

Easy upkeep in that it can be efficiently cared for.

Clothing for the elderly

Approximately half of the people over 65 years of age suffer from some form of physical handicap which affects the fitting of clothing, its appearance, and comfort to the wearer. The reason for needed clothing adaptations for the elderly is not age but rather the handicaps which in many cases accompany age.

Elderly people are stereotyped by society at large, often unfairly. The "careless appearance" stereotype takes for granted that older persons no longer care about their physical apppearance nor the impression their clothing has upon others. Stereotypes, however, are far from accurate. In general, elderly persons do care about their clothing, and desire a pleasing appearance which, if achieved, has a strong bearing on a positive self concept. The elderly wish to conform to current fashions, at least to the extent that they will be prevented from being singled out as different. An attractive appearance bolsters morale and self-assurance and greatly influences social acceptability. Clothing for the elderly should perform at least three functions for the wearer: accent or call attention to good points; camouflage poor ones; and give a psychological lift.

Physical changes which occur with advancing age can be seen as an asset or a liability. The older person can approach clothing selection with a healthy attitude using wise judgement to emphasize and accentuate good features. Changing hair color to gray and white, the softening of skin pigments, and wrinkling of the skin are changes which often add character and distinctiveness to elderly features and can be accentuated by color and line selection. Often the elderly find they cannot wear shades which were previously becoming. For them color selection is a whole new area with which to experiment. The elderly, however, are often conservative and do not readily accept colors and styles which they felt they could not wear when they were younger.

Changing figure proportions and problems with getting clothes which fit properly also accompany aging. The waistline and lower body tend to increase while folds of loose skin appear around the upper arms and in the chin and neck areas. Deposition of tissue in the upper back, and rounded shoulders also make accurate fit a problem. Older women, therefore, often prefer clothing with sleeves which cover the upper arms or are below elbow length. Generally, dresses with soft collars or a V-neckline which opens down the front and gored or A-line skirts, which allow ease of movement and cover the knees, are preferred.

Due to physiological changes, older persons are less able to adjust to extreme changes in temperature. As joints stiffen, clothing must be designed for ease of dressing and with closures adapted to decreasing dexterity of the fingers and failing eyesight. For these reasons, older women prefer front button or zipper openings and dresses with jackets for added warmth.

Older people tire easily and therefore clothing must be lightweight and require the minimal amount of energy to be donned and removed. Ease of care is also important— clothing which can be cleaned easily and requiring little or no ironing is desirable.

Safety in both the fabric and design of clothing is an important consideration. Loose, full garments may throw a person off balance or catch easily, while shoes without grips, or with dangling shoelaces, may present a hazard. Fire resistant fabrics are desirable, and care should be exercised in the choice of garment design and in its construction. Long, loose fitting sleeves are one of the worst fire and other accident hazards.

Clothing selection is affected by the social activity of the elderly as well as the money available to spend on clothing. Elderly people are often restricted financially in purchasing clothing, particularly due to a conservative taste, which cuts them off from much mass-produced merchandise, but then because their clothing lasts longer due to decreased physical activity this can often be offset to some extent. Social activity and clothing have a circular interaction. One depends on an attractive appearance to form initial social contacts while most social interactions demand acceptable clothing which is attractive and suitable to the occasion and the wearer.

The availability of clothing to the older consumer also poses a problem. Elderly people feel more independent and achieve personal satisfaction from personally selecting clothing. They often, however, have reduced access to shopping facilities since reduced energy and lack of transportation make shopping a strenuous activity. In addition, they may be handicapped by visual and hearing impairments, or unsteadiness on their feet, as well as finding sales people impatient and unwilling to give them the time and service they require.

Thus, when selecting clothing, elderly people must combine personal preference in clothing with styles which take into account their figure, physical abilities and limitations, social activities, and financial position. Many older people give priority to fit and style in the selection of clothing but comfort, price, ease of care, and warmth are factors also considered important.

In attaining a good fit, elderly people find that sizes in ready-to-wear are based on the standard measurements of younger people, and their figure changes are not taken into consideration. For example, waistlines are usually not large enough and the trend to straight lines, without a waistline seam, make pattern or garment alterations for figure faults more difficult. Most older women find that half sizes allow for more variation in figure types and are closer to providing the features they require. Generally the elderly require a shorter bodice and narrower shoulders in relation to large abdominal and hip width in clothes. The elderly also have difficulty in finding items which are no longer in vogue, but to which they have grown accustomed. An example of this is the unavailability in ready-to-wear outlets of certain brassieres and girdles designed for the mature figure.

Clothing for persons with limited finger dexterity and arm movement

Many persons are afflicted with arthritis and its allied disorders. Likewise, other crippling diseases such as multiple sclerosis affect many people. As these diseases and others progress, their victims develop difficulty in dressing and undressing.

Closures requiring fine hand coordination are among the most difficult. Velcro may be of help provided that it holds sufficiently and that fabric is used underneath the hook side of the Velcro so that it does not touch the skin and cause irritation. On a man's shirt, the buttons may be removed and sewn on top of the buttonhole with Velcro then being sewn underneath for closing. This restores the conventional appearance of the garment but makes it more serviceable.

Buttons on the cuffs of shirts, blouses, and dresses can be sewn on with elastic thread so that the hand can slide through without the need for unbuttoning. In general, garments with as few buttons as possible are desirable. This makes wrapped garments particularly appealing. Likewise, front closures are desirable in all garments from brassieres to slips, dresses, shirts, etc., since pulling a garment over the head may be a painful operation. Lined dresses make dressing easier since the need for a slip is eliminated.

For men, the front pocket alteration on trousers (p. 30) will help since the conventional appearance is retained yet the opening is made considerably more easily accessible with Velcro. For women, slacks have the advantage of keeping the wearer warm. Slacks with elastic waistbands will be easier to don since they stretch and no closure is necessary. Belt loops can be of great help in pulling the garment on.

Large zipper pulls, tassels, rings, and other additions may make the operation of a zipper easier. For the person whose arm movement is restricted, such as a stroke patient, a zipper may be added from the hem of the sleeve to the underarm, and a second one from the underarm to the hem of a jacket. If putting on mitts is a painful process a zipper may be added along the small finger side of the hand so that the mitt opens right out. Likewise, slippers may be made with a fine zipper along the back or along the top so that the foot can be positioned carefully and the slipper closed.

Action pleats and gussets, as well as raglan, kimono, and sleeves with deep square cut armholes, may help in cases where a person has problems in moving shoulders. A long fine zipper may be inserted along the center back of the blouse or shirt so that the back can be opened and the shirt or blouse made easier to put on. The zipper can be easily closed after the garment is worn if a string is passed through the zipper pull ahead of time.

Clothing for persons using crutches, or wearing braces or casts, and for the chairbound

All clothing is made for a person in a standing position, hence when worn by a person in a sitting position for any length of time, it will cause pulling and straining in certain places and will provide a surplus of fabric in others. If clothing is constructed at home, alterations can be made on the paper pattern before cutting the fabric (p. 97), thus yielding a more comfortable garment. Since sitting on folds of fabric will cause discomfort, jackets and capes can be easily shortened to seat level at the back. Slacks, skirts, and dresses can be altered so that the chairbound can dress and undress by themselves and at the same time are not sitting on bulky fabric. In this respect, back wrapped garments may help as the person need not sit on the back lapovers. Moderate fullness is recommended for both skirts and trousers for the person in the wheelchair. When fashion shows snug pant legs, undue strain is felt at the knee, causing discomfort. In those cases, the inseam of pants can be opened at the knee providing the necessary spread for comfort. Knit fabrics will help, as stretch will be made possible.

For the person with braces and casts, zippers inserted in the side seam or inseam of trousers will be useful, and belt loops will help the person dress by himself. Fashion today has produced wrapped pants which help conceal casts and braces and can be appropriate for any occasion.

The person wearing a brace or an amputee with a prosthesis will want to have some reinforcement to protect from rubbing—slacks can be lined or can be reinforced at appropriate points with fused-on fabrics or sewn-on patches of durable fabric. A detachable reinforcement such as a knee patch worn next to the brace, or a patch added to the right or wrong side of the garment, would receive the abrasion and extend the life of the garment. Applique or leather patches could be used to add fashion interest as well as reinforcement. If an invisible reinforcement is required, an iron-on patch can be applied to the inside of the garment. A layer of strong fabric may be set into the seam on the inside so that the reinforcement is not visible from the right side.

The person on crutches often finds that underarm seams and sleeves tend to pull and tear and be uncomfortable to wear. In such cases, sleeves with gussets, knit inserts, and action pleats will provide more room for arms to move. The open waistline seam (p. 93) will provide the vertical stretch required in using crutches. Long blouses, shirts, and overblouses will be comfortable since the tendency is for blouses to rise with the use of crutches.

Finally, a very real problem for the person in a wheelchair or the person on crutches is that of carrying things. Bags which fasten to wheelchairs and crutches, or bags which can be worn on the person are very useful. As well, belt pockets and change purse types of bags which are worn around the neck can become an asset since they can be worn with different garments.

Clothing for women
who have had mastectomies

Breast malignancy is the foremost cancer in women. A woman who has had a mastectomy may find that accepting her new self image is her most significant task. Reach for Recovery, which was founded in 1953, has been, since 1969, part of the service and rehabilitation division of the American Cancer Society. It publishes a small folder entitled a "letter to husbands," which tackles squarely one of a mastectomy patient's most profound fears: that her husband will no longer find her attractive.

Clothing can function to meet the needs of women who have had mastectomies. First it can restore the normal appearance as much as possible. This is best achieved by well fitting prostheses available in specialty shops and many large department stores. Information about these outlets may be obtained from most hospitals and cancer clinics. Available are bathing suits, lingerie, and loungewear with specially built-in bra cups or allowances for prostheses.

When fear has been allayed there's hope for development of a satisfactory self image of a woman attractive to her husband. Clothing should be selected, not only considering the woman's personal likes, but also those of the husband. This varies with individual tastes. For some, very dainty and feminine clothing may help in this respect. For others the more tailored, simple lines may be their preference. Women who have had mastectomies may have a swollen arm following the operation. Garments with kimono or dolman sleeves may be more comfortable to wear and may conceal this problem. The currently fashionable wide sleeves set into a deep cut armhole may also help, as well as garments with gussets.

To cope with the sunken area under the arm, an armhole shield made of any washable soft fabric and padded with polyester fiberfill may be pinned to the brassiere or slip.

"Don't neglect your appearance" is the advice given by Reach for Recovery to women who have had mastectomies. A mastectomy need not be a handicap since with a little care in selection of appropriate prostheses and suitable clothing its presence can be adequately concealed.

Clothing for the incontinent

Incontinence is the inability to control partially or wholly the action of the kidney, bladder, or bowel. It often occurs with aging at which time muscles slacken and lose their contractability or tightness. It should not, however, be credited solely to the aging process since there are people of all ages who suffer in varying degrees from this problem. Many young women experience a leaking bladder incontinence due to the failure of abdominal and uterine muscles to regain full tonicity after bearing children.

In general, people tend to be afraid of incontinence since they feel it demeaning to have this "lack of control" of their bodies and fear that old age is upon them. Depending on the severity of the incontinence, repair would conceivably range from an exercise program or minor surgery to major surgery and drainage of certain parts of the excretory system by the use of catheters or other appliances.

Any family doctor will discuss the needs of the patient and will inform him of the various medical suppliers from which ostomy supplies or supplies for incontinence may be purchased. The incontinent person will want to select clothing which is loose fitting so as to conceal any appliances or padding worn. Zippers on the inseam of trousers make for easy cleaning of urine bags which are taped to the leg. Likewise, gored skirts provide coverage and concealment of urine bags for women. The double half belt alteration (p. 28) on trousers for both men and women is ideal especially for the person with an ostomy. Lapped over back opening on nightgowns, dressing gowns, and skirts are particularly suitable for incontinence, since the lapped over sides may be pulled to each side when the person is sitting. For the chairbound woman who is also incontinent, housecoats and dresses may have the center back panel shortened to seat level, (p. 101).

Clothing for the blind

Blindness has three aspects to it: the physiological, the personal, and the social. Physiologically, blindness is most frequently the result of chemical and other changes in the organism. The personal experience of blindness and its implications are great, for not only is the person handicapped in his mobility but his sense of well-being is threatened and many adjustments need to be made in his approach to life. These adjustments affect his relations with others in his social group, and theirs with him.

The concept we have of ourselves determines to a great extent the clothes we choose and at the same time the clothing we wear influences both how we perceive ourselves and how we are perceived by others. The greatest problem the blind have with respect to clothing is choosing articles and shopping. Neither of these activities can be done independently of the assistance and tastes of others. Being fashionable presents difficulties in that fashion information cannot be obtained as readily by the blind as by the sighted. After the initial adjustment, care of clothing and organization of articles do not present insurmountable difficulties.

The blind person develops a keen sense of touch and therefore clothing can be identified by various differences in texture such as lace, rick-rack, braid, machine stitching, embroidery stitches, buttons, or braille tags. In purchasing clothing, the number of buttons or the placement of pockets can become the identifiable feature and consequently it is advisable never to buy two garments of the same style in different colors.

The blind person relies on other people telling him whether his appearance is pleasing or not. The reactions of others will help him to know that a certain style is attractive or that a specific color combination is pleasing. Sighted individuals can help the blind by commenting on various items of clothing: the suitability of certain styles and color combinations, for instance. In other words, sighted individuals can share their sight with the blind by talking to them about all aspects of clothing, fashion, and appearance.

Clothing for the obese

The results of Nutrition Canada's surveys indicate that in our society obesity may be considered a disease of epidemic proportions and that in some age groups as many as 87 percent are overweight. In recent years practitioners of various disciplines have conducted studies to identify the causes of and treatments for obesity. At the same time, with increased cardio-vascular illnesses, considerable attention has been directed to the role of normal weight and physical fitness in coping in a stressful environment. While there is little consensus on causes and treatments of obesity, results of all studies point to the health hazards that it presents and strongly recommend proper nutrition and maintenance of normal weight based on body build, height, sex, and age.

The age old concept that the fat person is an extroverted, happy-go-lucky, always-joking individual is far from correct. Studies relating to an individual's feelings about his body and about himself as a person show that the obese person often has a negative body image. The views which the obese holds about his body are frequently paralleled by an intense self-consciousness and even a misconception of how others view him. This is the point where clothing can play an important role for the overweight or obese individual.

For the overweight person clothing is more often than not a source of frustration since it poses several problems. In ready-to-wear clothing stores there is a limited range of sizes and very limited choice within large sizes. When extra large sizes appear there tends to be little fashion and color appeal to them. Pennington and Big 'n' Tall stores are retail outlets in the larger urban centers which carry large sizes in women's and men's wear respectively. Both are now attempting to provide a wider variety of color and styles for their customers. It is important, therefore, that obese men and women become very selective in choosing those clothing items that are most flattering and comfortable to them. Through a choice of clothing which makes him appear more slender, the obese person may gain a better self image. A new favorable reaction by spouse, children, and friends may help the obese person gain greater self confidence and may provide the dieter with the necessary incentive to stay on the weight reduction program. When clothing plays this role it is functioning in a very constructive manner for the wearer.

In clothing selection the elements of design which play a part in the total appearance of the wearer are line, space, color, texture, and pattern. These five components are blended in unique combinations and together create various effects on the human figure. The overweight person will want to select those combinations which make him appear more slender, yet combinations which are flattering; combinations which are comfortable to wear and which are to his liking.

Vertical lines make one appear taller and slimmer. The princess line and shirtwaist dresses, gently fitted, are classics and will add height to the figure. A narrow front panel makes the eye travel up and down. If a vertical line meets a horizontal line, as would be the case with a yoke on a dress, coat, or jacket, the eye is carried across and the person tends to appear shorter. A widening effect would also be caused by diagonal lines carrying the eye downwards, as by raglan sleeves. For this reason a set-in sleeve may be more flattering than a raglan sleeve on the overweight figure. If the diagonal lines carry the eye upward, as would be the case with the V-neckline, the person tends to appear taller and slimmer.

Advancing colors, such as red and yellow, can make an object seem closer and therefore larger, while the receding colors (those containing blue) make an object appear farther away and in turn smaller. Value (lightness or darkness) and intensity (brightness or dullness) also influence size. A bright vibrant blue will make one appear larger than a dark, grayed red. Black tends to make one appear smaller, but since it

clearly outlines the figure, it is not ideal for those with figure irregularities. Two-toned or multi-colored outfits divide the figure into definite parts thus adding width.

The manner in which a space is divided into areas by lines influences the appearance. A plain garment without a belt will be more slenderizing than one with a belt. Likewise if the belt is wide and of contrasting tones, the effect would be one of greater apparent width.

The effect of stripes on the figure varies depending on the width of the stripes and the space between them. Usually vertical stripes will make a person look taller and thinner, while horizontal stripes will make one appear shorter and wider. This rule, however, cannot be taken as an absolute since the effect can be totally reversed. It all depends on how your eye reacts to the width of the stripes and the distance between them on the fabric.

Prints make the figure look larger than a plain fabric in the same color. Usually designs of medium size with close color contrasts are the most flattering to any figure. Light and bright colors, sharp contrasts, and large motifs will increase one's apparent size while darker, blurred, overall patterns will decrease it. Motifs arranged in a vertical movement add height; horizontal ones will diminish it.

The surface or texture of a fabric can also influence apparent size. Glossy fabrics that reflect a great deal of light will make the figure appear larger, while dull surfaces tend to minimize size. Rough textured fabrics such as corduroy or nubby tweed, tend to appear bulkier than they really are and add pounds to the figure. Stiff fabrics can hide some body faults, but if one is big all over, stiff fabrics tend to make one look larger. Clingy fabrics in body hugging designs accentuate the shape. Draped effect and soft ties are flattering to most figures.

In summary, overweight men and women can select the combinations of line, color, space, texture, and pattern which make them appear more slender. It should be noted that through the interplay of these aspects of design one can compromise between the likes of the wearer and the most slenderizing effects. If a woman loves red but does not want to appear larger she can select a garment with vertical lines in a smooth soft fabric and in a dark dull red rather than a bright, vibrant one. Likewise, a man who likes plaids can use plaid in the trim on a jacket or in a tie rather than in a plaid suit or overcoat.

Sportswear for the handicapped

The functional aspects of dress which serve to establish a starting guideline for the selection of athletic sportswear for the handicapped are the following:

1. The garment should not impede mobility nor inhibit the movement requirements of the sport, such as:
    the flexing and extending of arms and legs;
    the extending of arms above the shoulders and head;
    the rotating and flexing of the neck;
    the use of pelvic and groin muscles;
    the extensive use of biceps and triceps;
    the rotation of the shoulders and the use of lower and upper back muscles.

2. The garment worn for wheelchair sports should be chosen to allow for the maximum use of the upper torso.

3. The garment should be durable— especially in areas of extensive wear such as the seat, knees, and elbows, to prevent fabric damage due to abrasion. Reinforcement should be used at points of wear.

4. The garment should be absorbent for comfort when perspiring. In this respect

natural fibers such as cotton and wool are good.

5. The garment should have low static electricity, since static increases soiling, and reduces the overall appearance. Synthetic fibers, such as nylon and polyester, tend to build up static electricity.

6. The garment should be easy to put on and take off as this can serve as a rehabilitative function in itself, and is most important at the onset of a disability.

7. The garment should be comfortable, taking into consideration the physical, psychological, and social dimensions of comfort.

In recent years, quite a number of handicapped people have become actively involved in sports that years ago were deemed out of reach for them. At the same time, great advances have been made in sportswear that features functional lines. Practicality appears to have filtered through to the designers and manufacturers to the degree that fashion follows functionalism. Emphasis on both function and fashion in construction and design has produced garments suited to anyone, and this has perhaps helped to dispel the idea of clothing specifically designed for the disabled and worn only by the disabled. Sportswear is making a very real contribution in this regard and many ideas found in sportswear can be adapted to other clothing as well, for both the able bodied and the disabled.

Maternity clothing

Today's fashions in maternity clothing provide a wide choice of well designed and expandable apparel. While pregnancy is a natural and normal process of life, the actual process of dressing during this period is made difficult because of the bodily changes which occur. Hence, pregnancy can be considered a temporary handicap. When one considers that pregnancy is a crisis period of life and that much anxiety during it is caused by ambivalent feelings, emotional concerns, feelings of inadequacy, and fear of rejection, one realizes the necessity of developing and maintaining high morale. An increase in psychological well being may be gained by an attractive appearance and since this is of importance and since clothes can contribute both to appearance and the feeling of confidence they should be more carefully selected during this period of life than at others.

Maternity clothing is usually designed to provide for six or seven added pounds at the time a woman begins wearing them, to 10 or 15 more before the pregnancy is over. Rapid expansion of abdomen and breasts occurs after the 26th week, and during the last two weeks the baby drops lower, thus lowering the waistline. Such physical changes require non-restricting clothing with expandable features; lightweight fabrics to maintain proper body temperature and with absorptive qualities to take care of increased perspiration. The basic selection criteria include attractiveness, comfort, and ease of care.

Style features considered to be fashionable and attractive are achieved by three different methods: conforming to the natural contours of pregnancy, camouflaging the middle contours, and focusing attention on the upper part of the body.

If a woman thinks that fashion for her is "conforming to natural body contours," it is taken for granted that she accepts her figure, and thus chooses styles that modify, but do not conceal natural lines, such as the bell, bubble, pyramid, or tent styles. To camouflage the middle contours, styles such as empire waists, skirts and jackets, pleats, folds, and gathers are worn. The styles that focus attention on the upper part of the body should incorporate vertical lines which lead the eye upward: unusual necklines, and accessories such as scarves and collars, or jewellery which emphasizes the neck and shoulders can be worn.

Basic design principles apply to maternity wear as to any other type of clothing. Figure type and proportion are a determining factor of the style. In color, most women do not deviate radically from the normal, although it is possible to take advantage of the short life of maternity clothes to experiment with unusual colors. If conservative colors are used as a background, colorful accessories may be added. Light colors tend to conceal a silhouette but make the person seem larger, whereas dark colors tend to reveal the silhouette but make one seem smaller.

Medical authorities recommend that maternity garments be suspended from the shoulder so as to have no restricting seams, and that it be designed for ease of dressing. The advantage of a two-piece outfit, however, is that expandable features are more easily incorporated while in a one-piece dress the front hemline tends to ride up as pregnancy progresses.

Fabrics should be easy to care for and lightweight so as not to cause fatigue. Separates, such as jumpers, can be worn with blouses and sweaters from the regular wardrobe in contrasting colors to direct attention to the upper part of the body, and can provide more variety than one-piece outfits.

Ideal fabrics for maternity wear have enough body to hold their shape. Dull textures tend to absorb light and conceal the size of the figure while surface interest or design relieves monotony. Stiff, bulky fabrics will add to the apparent size of the wearer. Examples of suitable fabrics include jersey, seersucker, double knits, chambray, corduroy, and gingham. Blends of natural and synthetic fibers tend to have the comfort aspects of natural fibers and the ease of care characteristics of the synthetics.

Textiles

The satisfaction gained from the purchase and use of any garment is determined by how well a garment performs relative to the consumer's expectations and predetermined preferences. Every individual has different priorities in terms of garment performance. Certain areas of textile performance are of major importance to those with physical handicaps. Outlined below are some general guidelines for achieving maximum personal satisfaction from textile products according to individual needs and priorities.

Durability

Synthetic or man-made fibers such as nylon and polyester tend to have superior qualities in the areas of yarn strength and fabric durability. They are generally more resistant to abrasion.

Blending a synthetic fiber and a natural fiber can utilize the superior durability qualities of the synthetic fiber and the superior absorbency and comfort of the natural fibers.

Tightly woven and knitted fabrics are usually stronger than those with a loose construction. In general, a woven fabric stands up to the friction of braces and other devices better than knitted fabrics. Knitted fabrics tend to snag, pull, and run under these conditions.

Shrinkage control finishes applied to natural fibers such as cotton, rayon, and wool extend the useful life of the garment. The same is true of water repellent, moth proof, and mildew resistant finishes.

Easy maintenance

An easy care garment is one which is machine washable with a maximum of wrinkle resistance. Most fibers, both man-made and natural, can be laundered successfully under domestic laundry conditions. Wool, acetate, spandex, and rubber are fibers which do not wash as successfully under machine washing conditions. Wool can be made machine washable if treated with a shrink resistant finish. The thermoplastic or heat sensitive man-made fibers such as acrylic or the olefins may not perform satisfactorily in a commercial or institutional laundry where very high temperatures are used. Wrinkle-resistant polyester and nylon garments may also be damaged by excessively high laundry temperatures. Certain novelty weaves with special surface effects, such as velvet, require drycleaning.

Tightly woven fabrics often wrinkle to a greater extent than weaves of moderate tightness and most knits. Wrinkle resistant and crease retention finishes have in many cases overcome the above problem, and may eliminate the need for ironing. Blending man-made and natural fibers often results in an easy care fabric. Wash-and-wear and soil release finishes have helped to reduce the amount of work associated with laundering clothing.

Absorbency

The absorbency of a fiber greatly influences the comfort of a fabric; the natural fibers, which absorb moisture readily, tend to "breathe" and regulate body heat. The synthetic fibers all have relatively poor absorbency; they tend to be hot if the atmosphere is warm, and cold when the atmosphere is cold. Fabrics such as cotton jersey are good choices if an individual is sensitive to heat and cold.

Static electricity build-up

Static electricity build-up is influenced by the degree of fiber absorbency. A synthetic fiber, with low absorbency, tends to readily accumulate static electricity resulting in shocks and a clinging fabric. Blends of a natural and synthetic fiber have been useful in decreasing or eliminating the static problem associated with man-made fibers, if not less than 35 percent of the total is the natural fiber. Chemical treatments to increase the anti-static and absorbency properties of fabrics have brought synthetic fibers closer to natural ones in terms of potential comfort.

Thermal insulation

Fabrics which can trap air provide good thermal insulation and warmth. Wool or acrylic fabrics that are bulky or have surface nap can trap air, making lightweight, warm garments. Garments need not be heavy to be warm.

Odor retention

Man-made fibers, especially polyester, hold body odors to a much greater extent than do the natural fibers. Anti-bacterial or bacteriostatic finishes are available and they inhibit the growth of a large group of bacteria, including odor-causing germs. These finishes may help to prevent the development and retention of body odors in garments. "Sanitized" is one such finish.

Allergies

Allergies to both natural and synthetic fibers are common. However, cotton seldom causes allergic reactions and is often the only feasible fabric choice.

Skin irritation

When skin irritation develops due to fabric rubbing, a solution is to reinforce the areas where the fabric contacts the skin with soft absorbent fabrics. In general, the less surface contact a fabric has with the body, the more comfortable is that fabric. Fabrics with raised surfaces such as cotton flannelette, terry toweling, and velour reduce the surface area in contact with the body.

Ease of dressing

The weight of a garment can be of great importance in terms of the amount of energy expended when dressing. Garment weight is influenced greatly by fabric construction and if weight is a problem, light weight fabrics should be chosen.

Stretch fabrics are easier to put on and take off than woven fabrics, with less tendency for seams to rip or fabric to tear. There is less need for an exact fit when a knit fabric is used, but there is the tendency for tight stretch fabrics to outline a brace or deformity.

Fabric design

Prints, overall designs, and textured fabrics can hide many figure variations. The type of dye or printing used on a fabric can influence its usable lifespan. Dyes which bleed, prints which wash off, and surface decoration such as flocking which is lost in cleaning, make a fabric unserviceable. No fool-proof generalization can be made for judging the probable fastness of dyes. If the color does rub off when the fabric is handled or stroked, it is likely to come off during wear and cleaning.

Comfort

Comfort is influenced by factors other than those resulting from fiber, yarn, and fabric properties. When choosing garments and fabrics these factors must also be taken into consideration.

Both style and fit influence the comfort afforded by the garment and comfort varies with individual preferences.

Choosing clothes and dressing according to certain habits affords a degree of comfort to the individual. Being accustomed to wearing a certain item of clothing, such as a girdle, may make it seem comfortable. The psychological adjustment required to go without such a clothing item could cause a high degree of discomfort. Habits should be considered when recommending clothing aids or changes to elderly or handicapped individuals.

A great deal of psychological comfort can be gained by being dressed as current fashion dictates. Most individuals greatly value independence in caring for their needs, and at all stages of life clothing should promote as much independence as possible.

Body sensitivity tends to increase with age and as this occurs, personal preferences change as to comfortable clothing. This change is usually in the direction of lightweight, soft fabrics, often with a raised surface.

Flammability

Children, elderly people, and individuals with slowed movements especially require protection from fire. It is essential that their clothing be made from fabrics of low flammability. Cellulosic fabrics are available with flame resistant finishes. These finishes lose their flame resistant properties when laundered with alkaline soap and hard water, or with non-phosphate built detergents in hard water. The flame retardancy can be maintained and restored by the use of a weak acid (vinegar in the rinse), use of a phosphate built detergent, or the use of a water softener either in the rinse or in the water system.

Good fiber and fabric choices to minimize the hazards of fire are:

Cottons and rayons with flame resistant finishes.

Wool fabrics.

Fabrics without surface nap.

Tightly woven fabrics.

Nylon and polyester are not highly flammable but if heated they may melt, resulting in skin burns.

Poor fiber and fabric choices in terms of flame resistance are:

Untreated cottons and rayons.

Acrylics, acrylic and cotton blends, and olefins.

Fabrics with a high degree of surface nap or pile.

Loose, open weaves.

Sewing instructions

3. All seam allowances are 16 mm (⅝ in) unless otherwise stated.

4. Enclosed seam allowances, such as those in a faced neckline, should be graded in layers of different widths to reduce fabric bulk. Generally, the garment seam allowance is left the longest.

5. When trimming corners, cut across the corner point to reduce bulk.

6. Clip the seam allowance of inner or concave curves to allow them to spread to a wider area.

1. The size of the scale patterns provided in this publication is for the average person. Pattern changes may be necessary to accommodate individual variations.

2. Grain is the lengthwise and crosswise direction of yarns in a fabric.
a. Lengthwise grain is parallel to the selvedge of a fabric. It is the strongest and **least** stretchy direction in a woven or knit fabric.
b. Crosswise grain is perpendicular to the selvedge. It is the **most** stretchy direction in a knit fabric.
c. Bias grain is a 45° angle between lengthwise and crosswise grain. In a woven fabric, the bias has the greatest stretch and least tendency to ravel.

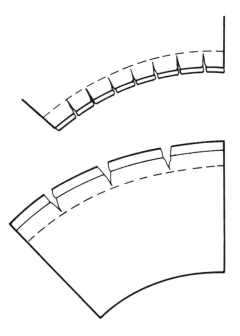

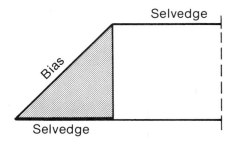

7. Notch or wedge the seam allowance of outer or convex curves to allow them to fit into a smaller area.

8. Understitching is a line of stitching 3 mm (⅛ in) from the seam, and through the facing and all seam allowances. Understitching prevents a facing or undercollar from showing on the right side of the garment.

Closures

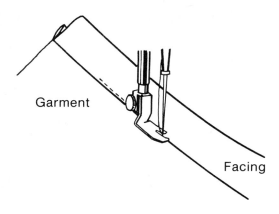

Garment

Facing

9. Topstitching is stitching on the right side of a garment, an even distance from a seam edge, fold, or zipper tape edge.

10. Belting is a stiffly woven fabric, available in various widths and weights.

11. Binding is a bias or straight strip of fabric which encases a garment edge and is visible from both the right and wrong sides. Binding for a curved edge must be cut on the bias; binding for a straight edge may be cut on straight grain or bias.

Fastening garments presents a special problem to individuals who have difficulty dressing. However, clothing may be adapted to use closures which are suited to the person's abilities. Generally a front closure is easier to handle.

Velcro
Velcro is a combination of hook tape and loop tape that lock together with a touch and is adjustable. Velcro is available in various widths and may be purchased by the centimeter or meter. It is also produced in

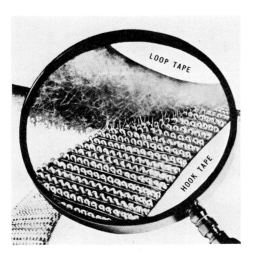

discs. Vel-Straps which are belts of Velcro with the hooked tape at one end and the belt portion made of the looped tape, are also available. These tapes are useful in forming easy to operate belts. Velcro may be used to replace buttons, hooks and eyes, and snaps. It is advisable that the hook tape, which can cause skin irritation, be placed so it will not come in contact with the body. Difficulties are that the hooks of the Velcro snag other fabrics, and lint collects between the hooks during laundering.

Buttons
Large, flat, round buttons which are greater than 16 mm (⅝ in) in width and with a raised edge, are usually considered easier to grasp and guide through buttonholes. As well, toggle buttons have received favorable evaluation by some handicapped people. Buttonholes should be sturdy and large enough for the button to slip through easily. Horizontal buttonholes tend to stay closed more readily than vertical ones. Buttons sewn with a long elastic shank rather than thread may allow the garment to be slipped on without being unfastened. A false button closing may be made by sewing Velcro between the front overlap and underlap and stitching the buttons on top of the buttonholes.

Buttonloops
Bias buttonloops or toggles which fit loosely over buttons are more convenient to fasten than are buttonholes. Elastic buttonloops stretch for easier fastening.

Zippers
If a zipper is desired, but fastening it is found difficult, the addition of a large pull tab or ring will make it easier to operate. The original pull tab may be enlarged by covering it with fabric to match the garment. A zipper topstitched to the right side of an article without a fabric overlap is less likely to catch fabric in its teeth. A novelty zipper with large, easily operated teeth, and a large pull tab, could be used to make a decorative feature of a necessary opening. Separating zippers are often useful when a complete opening is desired. Although invisible zippers may disguise an opening, they are often difficult to operate. Zippers are available in a wide variety of weights.

Gripper snaps
Some people may find that it is easier to exert the pressure required to fasten large gripper snaps than it is to fasten buttons which require manual dexterity.

Hooks and eyes
Large hooks and eyes provide a strong, invisible closure. Bathing suit hooks, covered fur hooks, and skirt hooks may be readily substituted for small hooks which are often difficult to manipulate.

Tie closures
A tie closure can usually be adjusted to accommodate body size. But if there is insufficient finger dexterity to fasten a tie, Velcro can be placed under a preformed knot to complete a belt type closure.

1. Trousers

Trousers with zipper in the side seam or inseam of the leg

Materials:
pair of trousers
55 cm (22 in) zipper
iron-on patch
60 x 10 cm (24 x 4 in) strip of fabric

A zipper inserted in the inseam of trousers may be helpful to a person who must wear an incontinence appliance. The same adaptation or a zipper inserted in the side seam may be useful for a person with a brace. In this case, an inside reinforcing patch may be sewn to the garment to protect the fabric from abrasion. For the person with a cast, an entire side seam may be closed with a separating zipper or better still with a two-way separating zipper. The latter would make it possible to open the side from the bottom up or from the waist down.

Instructions:
1. Remove stitching in inseam of trousers for the length of the zipper.

2. Insert zipper to open at hemline.

3. If a brace or artificial limb is worn, an iron-on patch will protect the fabric. Stitch around the edges of the patch for greater durability.

4. An insert may be needed to protect the skin from the abrasive action of the zipper. Fold the strip of fabric lengthwise, right sides together, and stitch across ends. Trim and turn. Stitch inset underneath zipper on one side, matching edge to zipper tape.

Zippers of any length may be inserted in the side seam of pants to facilitate dressing for a person wearing a cast or a brace.

Overall with side zippers

This pair of overalls has two long separating zippers in the side seams from waist to hem. The idea is adapted from warm up ski pants and would be useful for a person who has restricted movement or the person who needs assistance in dressing and undressing.

Pants with two front zippers

Pants with two zippers in the front, in line with the creases, are a current fashion item. The use of two zippers to hip level 22 cm (8½ in) below waist increases the size of the waist opening, making dressing easier for the person with limited body movement. This idea can be adapted, and long two-way separating zippers inserted from hem to waist, down the front crease line of men's or women's trousers. The pants can be opened out completely and placed on a chair to facilitate dressing a seated person.

Slacks with double waistbands and side zippers

The double waistbands and side zippers on trousers for men or women allow the front or seat of pants to be dropped separately so that the rest of the garment is held up in place and does not fall to the floor when the zippers are opened. This modification aids in the use of bathroom facilities and in meeting the needs of the incontinent person. The alteration can be done on ready made trousers or home sewn ones.

Materials:

two 30–45 cm (12–18 in) zippers
two strips of fabric 7 cm (2½ in) wide and the circumference of the waist plus 8 cm (3 in) extra in length for overlap. If trouser fabric is not available use grosgrain ribbon in matching color for both front and back waistbands.

Instructions:

1. Remove waistband and open side seam of pants to the length desired for the zipper.

2. Insert zippers into the side seams, so they open at the waist.

3. Construct two waistbands, each to fit the circumference of the waist with a 4 cm (1½ in) overlap.

4. Stitch one waistband to pants front, leaving the band free at the back. Apply Velcro to fasten the ends at center back.

5. Stitch second waistband to pants back, leaving the band free at the front. Apply Velcro to fasten the ends at center front.

Note: The bands may also be made out of contrasting fabric to simulate a belt.

On men's trousers it is simpler and more inconspicuous if the waistband is not removed but rather slashed at the sides. In such a case, follow these instructions:

1. Cut through waistband and open side seams of pants to the length desired for the zipper.

2. Insert the zippers into the side seams below the waistband, so they open at the waist.

3. Bind the cut edges of the waistband with bias tape to finish the raw edges.

4. To the waistband at side fronts of pants attach a strip of grosgrain ribbon at each side sufficient in length to fit around the waistline at the back and provide an overlap of 4 cm (1½ in).

5. Stitch a 4 cm (1½ in) Velcro strip to ends of grosgrain ribbon to fasten at the back.

6. To the waistband at side backs of pants attach a strip of grosgrain ribbon at each side sufficient in length to fit around the waistline at the front and provide an overlap of 4 cm (1½ in).

7. Stitch a 4 cm (1½ in) Velcro strip to ends of grosgrain ribbon to fasten at the front.

Front pocket alteration on men's trousers

The front of men's pants can be altered at the front side pockets to make a front flap which retains the conventional appearance. This aids in the use of bathroom facilities and adjustment of appliances. It is particularly suitable for the person with limited finger dexterity who is unable to manipulate a zipper or buttons and buttonholes.

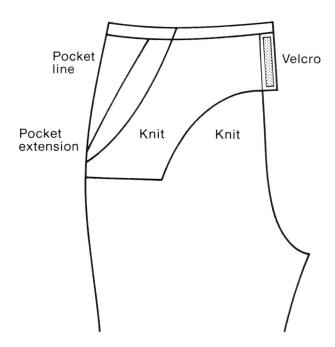

Pocket line

Velcro

Pocket extension

Knit

Knit

Materials:
men's pants
8 cm (3 in) Velcro
0.45 m (½ yd) sturdy lightweight knit fabric

Instructions:
1. Cut through the waistband at the top of both pockets and remove the part of the pocket that is lining fabric.

2. Cut a narrow strip from the pocket facing and bind the raw edges of the waistband.

3. From the knit fabric, cut an inside facing and waistband as shown in the diagram.

4. Stitch inside knit facing to edge of pocket and waistband.

5. Stitch Velcro to fasten inside facing at center front and front flap to waistband.

Pants
with one wrap-around leg

Trousers with one lapped side seam are suitable for a person wearing a long leg cast which limits the ease of bending and consequently the ease of putting on pants.

Materials:
2 m (2 yd) of 150 cm (60 in) fabric (approx.) approximate size pants pattern
10 cm (4 in) Velcro

Instructions:
1. Lay the front and back pattern pieces flat. Position the pieces together, matching seamlines and the hip and keeping the straight of grain of both pattern pieces parallel. The seamlines will not match below this point, nor where the side seam curves from hip to waist.

2. To form the pattern for the back of the wrapped leg, trace on the cutting line of the joined pattern from center back to halfway between the original side seam and center front (A). Join the waist and hem with a line on straight grain (AB).

3. A dart is needed at the side seam position to give the shaping normally provided by the seam. Trace the gap between front and back pattern pieces from hip to waist to form the dart.

4. Repeat steps 2 and 3 for the pants front, tracing from center front to halfway between the side seam and center back (CD).

5. The waistband will open at the wrapped side. Extend the waistband front and back at the side seams the length of the wrap-around extension at the waist.

6. Cut one regular front and back pant leg and one extended front and back. Cut waistband.

7. Press edges of front and back wrap-around extensions under 13 mm (½ in) and topstitch in place.

8. Construct body of pants as usual, the only difference being that the wrapped side seam is left open.

9. Attach waistband to pants. Fasten with Velcro.

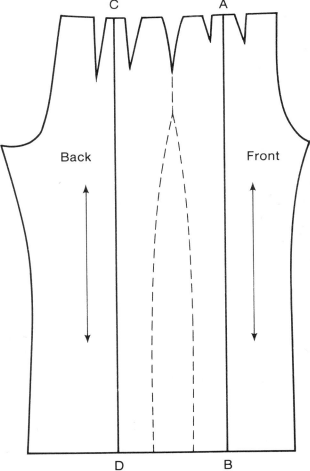

In every fashion season, some styles are particularly suited to the needs of a physically disabled person. Pants for women are currently fashionable for all occasions and provide warmth, modesty, and freedom of movement. Variations include easy-fitting drawstring pants, jumpsuits, and gaucho pants which may resemble a skirt.

Vogue pattern no. 9496

Vogue pattern no. 9536

Vogue pattern no. 7906

Wrap-around pants

Wrap-around styles have the advantage of being easily put on and taken off. To accommodate dressing in a wheelchair, a front wrap garment can be placed in the wheelchair before the person is seated. Garments which wrap in the back can be arranged so that a chair-bound person need not sit on folds of fabric. Wrapped garments can be fastened with ties, Velcro, buttons, or hooks depending on the finger dexterity and degree of arm movement of the individual.

The wrapped pants illustrated are lapped at each side seam so that the garment opens out flat. This would aid in dressing and concealing a cast or brace.

Front wrap gaucho pants

Below-knee-length gaucho pants offer comfort and modesty for a chair-bound person. A Velcro closure on the wrap for opening facilitates dressing for those with limited finger dexterity. Instructions overleaf.

Materials:
gaucho pants pattern
fabric as required
two Velcro discs
tape or ribbon for tie belt

Instructions:
1. To convert a standard gaucho pants pattern to a wrapped style, extensions must be added to both sides of the center front seam. Sketch an extension onto the left front to form a smooth curve (AB) from crotch to side waistline. To form the underlap on the right side, draw a line perpendicular to straight of grain from A to C, 8 cm (3 in) long. Continue from this point in a smooth curve to the waistline (CB). Add length to the waistband to correspond with the front extensions.

2. Cut out patterns.

3. Stitch darts, side seams, and inseams.

4. Stitch crotch seam from back waistline to point D.

5. Finish raw edges of extension pieces.

6. Attach waistband.

7. Attach Velcro discs to hold the ends of each extension in place at the waistband.

8. Hem pant legs.

9. A belt can be stitched to the back waistband and tied in front.

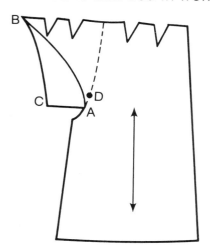

Tie-on garments

Slacks and jumpsuits can be made with a back wrap or a front wrap. Several commercial patterns for these are currently available.

Butterick pattern no. 4916

Drop seat jumpsuit

This jumpsuit has a horizontal waistline back opening with 30 cm (12 in) zippers on either side. The back waistline opening is fastened by means of snaps or Velcro and covered with a belt. The advantage of the drop seat is that the jumpsuit is easier to put on since the back of the garment can spread. When a person wishes to go to the bathroom, the whole garment does not need to be removed.

Wrap-around garments are usually fastened by tying. This may be easier to manage than buttons or zippers. A tie closure has the added advantage of being adjustable to fit variations caused by body shape and required appliances.

Materials:
ready-made jumpsuit or commercial pattern
and fabric for jumpsuit
two 30 cm (12 in) zippers
6 snaps or Velcro discs

Instructions:
Constructing a jumpsuit
1. Leave the back waistline seam and the trouser side seams open for 32 cm (13 in).

2. Fold under the seam allowances of the bodice and trousers at the back waistline, and stitch.

3. Insert zippers in the side seams.

4. Apply snaps or Velcro to keep back waistline seam closed.

5. A wide belt will cover the back opening.

Altering a jumpsuit
1. If jumpsuit has a waistline seam, remove stitching in back waistline and for 32 cm (13 in) in the trouser side seams. Proceed as above.

2. If the jumpsuit does not have a waistline seam, slash horizontally across the back at the waistline and remove stitching in trouser side seams to accommodate zippers. Bind raw edges at waistline. A belt will cover the bound edges. Proceed as above.

Pant jumper

A pant jumper style is advantageous for ease of movement and modesty. A front zipper and drop seat simplifies dressing and use of bathroom facilities.

Materials:
commercial pattern for pant jumper
required fabric plus 0.4 m (½ yd)
zipper 40 cm (16 in)
28 cm (11 in) of 4 cm (1¼ in) elastic—or to fit size of wearer's waist from side to side across the back.
package of 2.5 cm (1 in) twill tape.

Instructions:
1. The back pattern piece needs to be cut in two pieces for the drop seat. Cut the pattern perpendicular to center back, approximately 18 cm (7 in) below the waistline. Curve this line higher at center back as shown on the pattern AB. The center back seam of the upper back may be placed on the fold. Extend the lower pattern piece 7.5 cm (3 in) up from waistline. Cut on CD.

2. Cut two pieces of fabric 51 cm (20 in) long and 7 cm (2½ in) wide for the ties.

3. Insert zipper in front seam.

4. Dart the upper back as the pattern directs. Finish lower edge of upper back.

5. Stitch center back seam of lower back.

6. Stitch elastic to the wrong side of fabric at the upper edge of back flap. Fold under 5 cm (2 in) so elastic is concealed, and topstitch at edge of elastic.

7. Fold ties in half lengthwise, right sides together. Stitch side and one end of ties. Trim seam and corners, turn to right side. Attach ties to end of the elastic at sides.

8. Stitch twill tape to edge of drop seat flap, covering the ends of elastic and ties.

9. Insert belt loops for the ties in the side seam at the waist.

10. The ties are knotted in front to hold the drop seat in place.

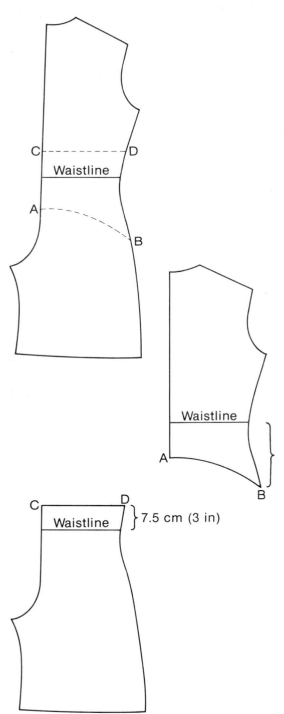

Tie panel jumpsuit

This jumpsuit utilizes the dropped seat idea.
The back seat panel is extended to tie in
the front.

44

Jumpsuit with hip zipper

A jumpsuit with both a vertical front opening
and a hip level horizontal zipper makes it
easier to dress and to fulfil bathroom
requirements. From the front, the hip zipper
may be partly concealed by pockets stitched
to the upper part of the garment. Instructions
overleaf.

Materials:

jumpsuit with front opening
zipper, 8 cm (3 in) less in length than the circumference of the jumpsuit at the hipline
strip of fabric 10 cm (4 in) wide and the length of the zipper plus seam allowances

Instructions:

1. Baste the zipper onto the right side of the jumpsuit at hip level.

2. Topstitch along edges of zipper tape, leaving ends unfastened.

3. On wrong side of jumpsuit, slash through fabric underneath zipper teeth to within 2.5 cm (1 in) of end of stitching. At this point, slash diagonally to ends of stitching to form a triangle.

4. Turn ends of zipper and triangle at ends of slash to the inside, and stitch through zipper tape and triangle, at ends of horizontal rows of stitching, from the wrong side. Do not stitch through to right side of garment.

5. Trim fabric underneath zipper tape to 3 mm (⅛ in) from stitching.

6. An inset is needed to protect the body from the abrasive action of the zipper. Fold the strip of fabric, right sides together, and stitch both ends. Trim and turn.

7. Baste inset underneath zipper, matching raw edges to upper edge of zipper tape. Topstitch along previous line of stitching, through zipper tape and inset.

Jumpsuit with scooped out seat for chairbound

A jumpsuit with a wrap-around bodice back and scooped out seat allows a person sitting in a wheelchair to be dressed without having to be lifted.

Materials:
jumpsuit pattern to fit
fabric as required plus 0.50 m
10 Velcro discs
1.60 m (1¾ yd) double-fold bias tape

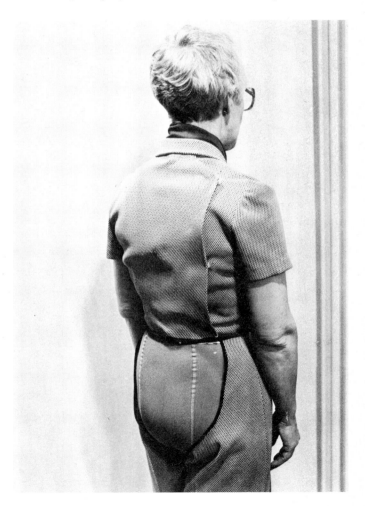

Instructions

Pants

1. Scoop out the seat of the pants by drawing a curved line beginning at the waistline, 5 cm from the side seam and ending 5 cm from the crotch point. The result will be a wide U-shaped scoop removed from the seat area.

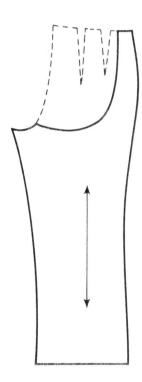

2. Construct pants as usual with center back seam extending only to 5 cm from the crotch point. Bind raw edge of scoop with double-fold bias tape.

Right bodice

1. Add a 5 cm (2 in) extension at center back.

2. Construct right bodice back as the pattern directions suggest.

3. Fold extension to right side and stitch neck edge of bodice and extension together using 16 mm (⅝ in) seam allowance. Grade and clip, then turn the extension to the wrong side of bodice and press.

Left bodice

1. Trace a second bodice back pattern and tape the two patterns together at center back to form a complete back.

2. Draw a line parallel to and 3 cm (1¼ in) below shoulder seam on right bodice back (ab). From a point on this line 5 cm (2 in) from the armhole, extend a line to the waistline 5 cm (2 in) from the side seam (bc). This line forms the finished shape of the back bodice.

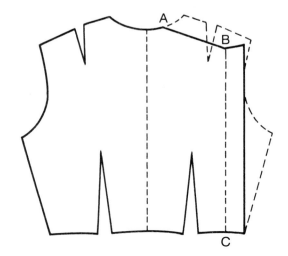

3. Add a 15 mm (⅝ in) seam allowance to the shoulder edge of the overlap.

4. To form a facing, fold paper back on the finished edge of overlap. Draw a parallel line 5 cm (2 in) from the finished edge. Trace edge of overlap at shoulder and waist to join parallel lines. Press pattern flat.

5. Cut out left bodice using the pattern.

6. Construct left bodice as the directions suggest. Press left waistline dart to center back and the overlap waistline dart toward the right side seam.

7. Fold facing and bodice right sides together. Stitch upper edge using a 15 mm (⅝ in) seam allowance. Grade, then turn the facing to the wrong side of bodice and press.

8. Attach Velcro discs at neck edge, center back, and edge of overlap to hold bodice back in place.

Attaching pants & bodice

1. Join pants and bodice at waistline to the point where pants seat is removed.

2. Cut off 15 mm (⅝ in) seam allowance of bodice at opening of the U. Bind raw edge of bodice with double-fold bias tape.

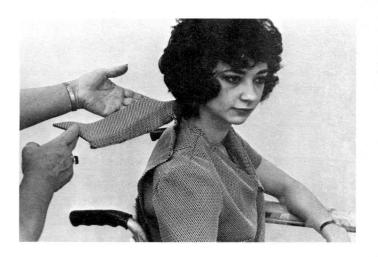

Neckline

Any type of neckline is suitable for a wrap-around back bodice.

If the pattern does not have a collar, use the new back pattern as a guide to draft a new back facing which includes the overlap.

If the pattern has a collar, use the regular collar pattern.

1. Attach the collar to the left side of the garment as instruction sheet directs.

2. Clip collar neckline 15 mm (⅝ in) at the point where the overlap ends.

3. Zig-zag seam allowances of remaining portion of upper and under collar together.

4. Attach Velcro discs to neckline of under collar.

5. Face right neckline of garment with double-fold bias tape *pressed open*. Top stitch loose edge of bias tape to garment.

6. Attach Velcro discs to facing so that collar will lay flat when wrapped around the neck and fastened.

Pants with a back flap

Pants with a back vertical flap can be put on while the person is seated, and they make toilet requirements easier. The wrap-around flap prevents exposure when the person is standing.

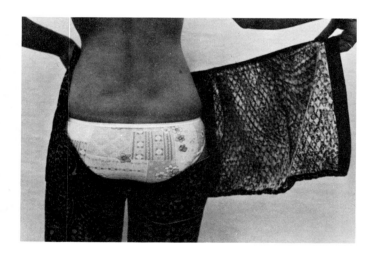

Materials:
pair of pants
45 x 70 cm (18 x 28 in) piece of fabric similar to the pants
38 cm (15 in) Velcro
90 cm (1 yd) double-fold bias tape
2.5 cm (1 in) elastic, half the circumference of the individual's waist
60 cm (24 in) of 6 mm (¼ in) elastic

Instructions:
1. Cut seat out of pants beginning 4 cm (1½ in) from the side seam and cutting in a U-shape to 10 cm (4 in) above crotch points or approximately 46 cm (18 in) below waist (see photo 1).

2. Bind cut edge with double-fold bias tape.

3. Cut the seat flap using original garment piece as a pattern so that the center back seat curve remains the same. Add sufficient width for the seat flap to reach the side seam.

4. Construct the flap as if it were the back of a pair of pants, i.e., center back seam, pockets, waistband.

5. Fold under a 2 cm (¾ in) hem and stitch along edge to form a casing. Thread narrow elastic through casing, tightening it to fit the individual.

6. Stretching slightly, apply 2.5 cm (1 in) elastic to upper edge of flap to form a back waistband.

7. Open right side seam to 35 cm (14 in) below the waist. Insert right side of flap into the seam and restitch the seam.

8. Stitch Velcro to edge of flap and left side seam to fasten the flap in place.

Note: The length of the flap varies with the individual's size and build. 32–36 cm (13–14 in) is the length required for an average adult man.

2. Shirts, blouses, and sleeve adjustment

Shirt with back opening

A shirt which can be opened in the back as well as in the front makes dressing easier for a person with limited arm movement.

Materials:
shirt
10 cm (4 in) matching fabric
55 cm (22 in) lightweight zipper

Instructions:
1. Remove stitches in collar at center back neck edge for about 4 cm (1½ in).

2. Place zipper, right side up, on right side of center back. The zipper should open from bottom to top, with the ends of the zipper tape extending into the collar through the opened seam. The lower ends of the zipper tape should be turned under 6 mm (¼ in).

3. Topstitch along edge of zipper tape.

4. On wrong side of shirt, slash through fabric underneath zipper teeth.

5. Fold cut edge under so that folded edge is 1 cm (⅜ in) from zipper teeth. Topstitch again to enclose raw edges.

6. An inset is needed to protect the body from the abrasive action of the zipper. Fold a 55 x 5 cm (22 x 2 in) strip of fabric in half lengthwise, right sides together. Stitch ends. Trim and turn. Finish raw edges of inset.

7. Baste inset underneath zipper, matching raw edges to left side of zipper tape and extending inset into opened collar seam. Topstitch through shirt, zipper tape and inset, on previous line of stitching.

8. Restitch collar seam.

Note: A similar back closure can be constructed using 5 snaps or 5 Velcro discs. An overlap and underlap must be constructed from additional matching fabric.

Snap-top shoulder seam

An opening from sleeve hem to neckline provides a blouse with a wide opening, simplifying dressing for a person with restricted arm movement. The opening is fastened with snaps.

This modification can be done whenever the bodice and sleeve are cut in one as would be the case with a kimono sleeve or raglan sleeve, provided the front and back of the raglan sleeve are in separate pieces.

Snap-crotch
man's sports shirt

This shirt is commercially produced and sold for sports wear. While this type of shirt has been on the market for women it is relatively new for men.

A handicapped person may, depending on the disability, find this useful in that the shirt would stay down. In addition, since handicapped individuals are more and more active in sports, it may prove valuable to them.

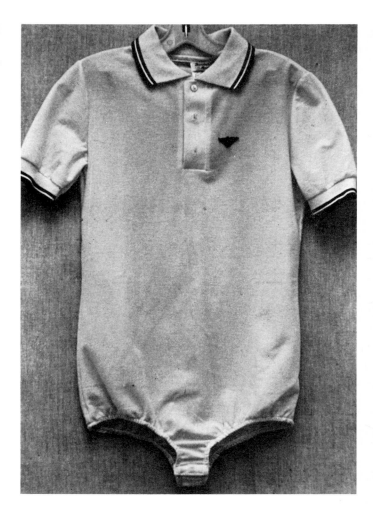

Cross-over neckline

It is often difficult for a person whose body movements are restricted to get a garment with a close-fitting neckline over the head. Fasteners on a larger neck opening may be difficult to handle. A cross-over neckline combines a large opening for easy dressing with a close-fitting appearance.

Front cross-over neckline

Materials:
commercial pattern with yoke above bustline
fabric as required plus 0.25 m (¼ yd)

Instructions:
1. From the original pattern sketch a new front neckline curve so that the fabric overlaps 10–15 cm (4–6 in) at the yokeline. (For added room a similar change can be made in the back neckline if there is also a back yoke).

2. Cut two identical front yoke pieces and remainder of pattern as directed.

3. Stitch shoulder seams.

4. Finish neckline using binding or facing.

5. Overlap the front yoke pieces, baste in place, and attach to bodice front.

6. Complete the garment as the pattern suggests.

Envelope neckline

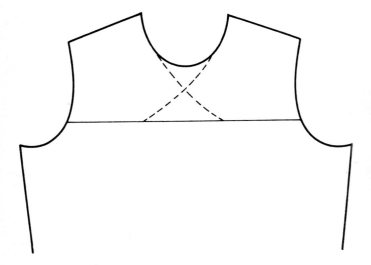

Instructions overleaf

Materials:
commercial T-shirt pattern
fabric as required plus 0.15 m (⅛ yd)

Instructions:

1. Pin bodice front and back patterns together at shoulder seam.

2. Draw new front and back neckline and shoulder seams as in diagram. Raise front and back neckline 2.5 cm (1 in) at center front and center back. Overlap the shoulder seams 10 cm (4 in) at the armhole.

3. Finish the neck edge of the garment.

4. Overlap the neckline at the shoulder, and baste in place.

5. Construct the T-shirt following the pattern instructions.

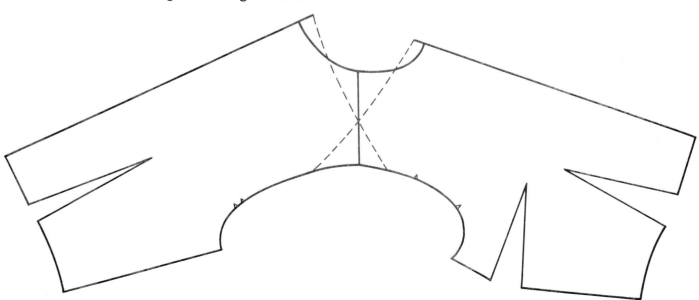

Raglan sleeve T-shirt

To aid in putting a T-shirt over a person's head, zippers can be inserted into raglan sleeve seams.

Materials:
T-shirt with raglan sleeves or fabric and notions to make T-shirt
two 22 cm (9 in) zippers
two 8 x 26 cm (3 x 10¼ in) strips of lightweight knit fabric

Instructions:
Hand-made T-shirt
1. Cut front raglan sleeve seam allowances 16 mm (⅝ in) wide. Cut neckband in two sections, cutting the band at each front raglan sleeve seam and adding seam allowances.

2. Construct body and sleeves of T-shirt, leaving front raglan sleeve seams open.

3. Match one edge of neckband, right sides together, to neckline in back and front, and stitch.

4. Machine baste front raglan sleeve seam closed.

5. Center zipper with teeth under basted seam, folding top of zipper tape underneath, and baste into position.

6. Topstitch from right side around zipper at 6 mm (¼ in) from seam. Remove basting.

7. A fabric inset is needed to protect the body from the abrasive action of the zipper. Fold the strip of fabric lengthwise, right sides together, and stitch ends. Trim and turn. Sew

the inset to the sleeve seam allowance so that it extends forward between the zipper and the body.

8. Turn neckband to the inside along the foldline, covering the ends of the zipper tape. Stitch in the well of the seam from the right side to fasten the neckband.

Ready-made T-shirt
1. Remove stitching in front raglan sleeve seams and cut through neckband.

2. Press 6 mm (¼ in) seam allowance under along opening, tapering to underarm seam.

3. Place bottom of zipper at underarm seam, then baste zipper into the open seam leaving the zipper teeth exposed. Use a zipper foot to stitch around the zipper at 1.5 mm (¹⁄₁₆ in) from the zipper teeth.

4. A fabric inset is needed to protect the body from the abrasive action of the zipper. Follow above procedures (Step 7) for inset, but stitch inset to zipper tape.

The raglan sleeves of a dress or blouse can be treated in the same way.

Blouse with bias back extending into sleeve

A garment with a set-in sleeve may not have enough moving ease for a person who must use crutches or a wheelchair. The back bodice is placed on the bias and extended into the sleeve to reduce binding of the armhole.

Materials:
commercial pattern with set-in sleeves
fabric as required

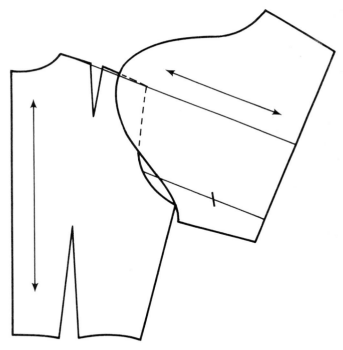

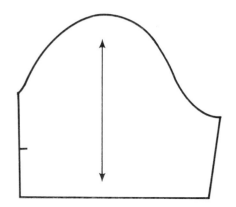

Instructions:

1. Join sleeve and back bodice of pattern as follows: Match center grainline of sleeve to shoulder seam. Maintaining grainline, lap sleeve cap over shoulder seam until cutting lines of sleeve and underarm match. Draw a line parallel to sleeve grainline through the armhole notches. Tape sleeve to armhole below parallel line.

Cut sleeve pattern apart on this line, leaving the lower sleeve joined to the bodice back. Bodice upper armhole and the remainder of the sleeve are unchanged. If the sleeve meets the underarm seam below the original underarm point, length will be subtracted from the back side seam. Add a compensating amount evenly to the hemline of the bodice back. Add 16 mm (⅝ in) seam allowance to center back seam. In order that the bodice front matches the altered bodice back, raise the front notch on the side seam an equal amount.

2. Cut out the garment, being sure to place the bodice back on the bias.

3. Stitch darts and shoulder seams. Press.

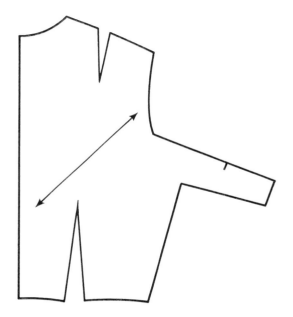

4. Ease sleeve cap to fit bodice armhole, and stitch.

5. Stitch upper sleeve to under sleeve.

6. Stitch underarm seam.

7. Complete garment as the pattern directs.

64

Many types of T-shirts and golf shirts featuring gussets and other unusual sleeve treatments can be found now in clothing stores. These provide greater freedom of movement.

Shirt or blouse
with underarm gusset

A gusset may be added to the underarm of a sleeve for greater moving ease. Because the area under the arm receives a maximum amount of strain and needs to stretch, the gusset should be cut on the bias.

Materials:
0.20 m (¼ yd) fabric to match garment blouse or shirt with set-in or raglan sleeve

Instructions:
The gusset may be added to a garment with a set-in or raglan sleeve.

1. Cut a 10–15 cm (4–6 in) square of fabric on the bias.

2. Remove stitching for 7–10 cm (2½–4 in) in underarm seams. See Diagram 1.

3. Fold garment fabric to inside between ABCD and press. See Diagram 2. Trim off triangles leaving a 16 mm (⅝ in) seam allowance.

4. Position bias square on inside of garment underneath the opening. Baste in place.

5. Topstitch from the right side of the garment 3 mm (⅛ in) from turned edge. See Diagram 3.

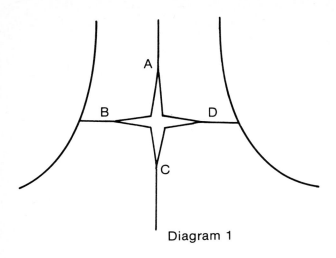

Diagram 1

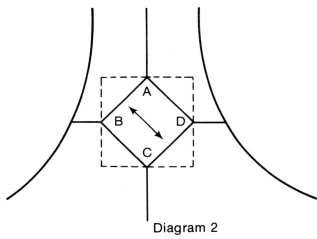

Diagram 2

Blouse or shirt with pocket gusset

A pocket gusset in the back of the armhole, similar to those found in uniforms, will increase moving ease for persons on crutches or in wheelchairs. Instructions overleaf.

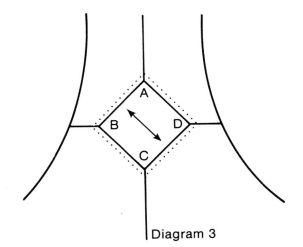

Diagram 3

67

Materials:

0.30 m (⅓ yd) fabric to match garment
garment with set-in sleeve

Instructions:

1. Open back of sleeve seam from 2.5 cm
(1 in) below shoulder seam to the underarm
seam.

2. To prepare pocket gusset pattern, trace
the shoulder seam and armhole curve from
the bodice back. From position A on the
shoulder seam, which is 7 cm (2¾ in) from the
sleeve cap, draw a line on the straight of
grain to B, 7 cm (2¾ in) below the underarm
curve. Draw a perpendicular line to C, at
the side seam.

3. Cut two gusset pieces.

4. Fold sleeve and bodice together so that
sleeve seam is flat. Place both gusset pieces,
wrong sides together, between sleeve and
bodice, matching curves. Stitch one gusset to
lower sleeve curve and one to bodice armhole
curve.

5. Turn gusset to inside so that it does not
show.

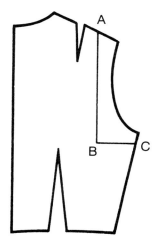

6. Clip and understitch bodice seam.

7. Stitch gusset pieces together on the inside
and lower edges.

8. Stitch ends of gusset inset to bodice
shoulder and side seams.

Dress with
back action pleats

Action pleats in the back of a dress, similar to those found in uniforms, will add moving room for a person using crutches, a walker, or a wheelchair.

Materials:
dress with set-in sleeves
0.45 m (½ yd) matching fabric

Instructions:
1. Remove stitches in back of sleeve from shoulder to 5 cm (2 in) past underarm seam in front.

2. Remove stitches in bodice underarm and back waistline seams.

3. On wrong side of bodice back, draw a line parallel to straight of grain from armhole, 3 cm (1¼ in) below shoulder, to waistline seam. Slash bodice back apart on this line.

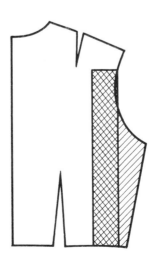

4. Trace side bodice piece on a piece of paper. Add a 10 cm (4 in) extension along the straight edge, thus increasing the width of the side bodice piece. Continue the armhole curve to join the top of the extension. Cut a side bodice using this new pattern.

5. To form a facing for the back bodice, cut a 10 cm (4 in) strip of fabric on the lengthwise grain. The facing will be the same length as the extension which was added to the side back.

6. Stitch the facing to the bodice back, using a 5 mm (¼ in) seam allowance. Understitch the seam and press the facing to the underside of the bodice back.

7. Stitch the side bodice panel to the bodice front at the underarm.

8. Sew the edge and top of the side back extension to the facing to form a pleat.

9. Topstitch the bodice back at the bottom edge of the pleat to the side bodice for 10 cm (4 in) to hold the pleat closed at the waistline.

10. Rejoin bodice to skirt on the original waistline seam.

11. Insert the back of the sleeve into the armhole again, incorporating the top of the pleat in the seamline at 5 cm (2 in) from the shoulder.

Bias panel blouse
(10 cm [4 in] bias panel)

The bias panel extending from the lower hem of the blouse through to the sleeve gives freedom of movement to the person on crutches or in a wheelchair.

Materials:
blouse pattern
fabric as required, plus 0.60 m (⅔ yd)

Instructions:

1. To obtain a pattern adjusted to accommodate the 10 cm (4 in) panel, trim 5 cm (2 in) from the sides of the pattern pieces for the bodice front, bodice back, and from both sides of the sleeve. (The side bust dart will be shortened and the elbow dart may be eliminated as ease).

2. Cut a bias piece of material the total length of the underarm through to the hem of the blouse. Insert the panel.

3. Finish blouse as directed.

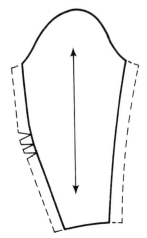
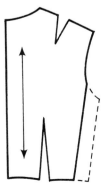

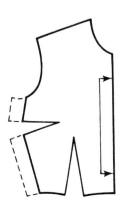

Dress with surplice cuff

Wide sleeves are comfortable because they do not restrict movement. The sleeves, however, may pose a threat to safety if the lower edge is free to catch on objects. The wide opening may be tightened by adding a surplice cuff, thus retaining the comfort, but reducing the hazard.

Materials:
garment with wide sleeves
0.20 m (¼ yd) fabric for cuff

Instructions:
1. Determine the circumference of the lower sleeve (A on diagram below).

2. Determine the circumference of the arm just below the elbow when the elbow is bent and add 5 cm (2 in) to this measurement for overlap (B on diagram).

3. Draw a pattern for the cuff in the shape of quarter moon. The depth of the cuff will be approximately 8 cm (3 in) , depending on the width of the sleeve. Cut out four cuff pieces.

4. With right sides of two cuff pieces together, stitch along edge B, using a 6 mm (¼ in) seam allowance. Clip and grade seam allowance, turn, understitch, and press. Machine baste raw edges together.

5. Fold sleeve in half lengthwise. Fold front half again, and mark the quarter point C on the lower edge of the front half of the sleeve.

6. Stitch A onto the lower edge of the sleeve so that the surplice cuff overlaps 5 cm (2 in) at quarter point C of the sleeve.

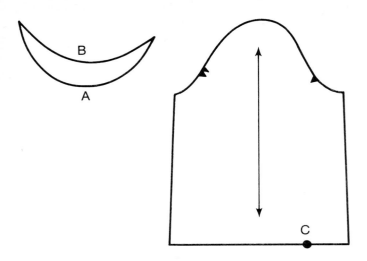

Vogue pattern no. 9216

Sleeves are a particular concern to those persons using a wheelchair or crutches. Dolman and raglan sleeves are usually less binding than set-in sleeves. Wide, three-quarter length sleeves with a dropped shoulder line are also comfortable. A ruffled shoulder area or strap may serve to hide a back deformity or a Milwaukee brace.

The current trend for men is toward more casual and loose-fitting garments which are less constricting than the traditional suit. This is a great help to handicapped men since the new fashions offer comfort which the traditional styles did not.

McCalls pattern no. 4745

Vogue pattern no. 1462

Petal sleeve

The petal sleeve is an attractive way to increase ease in a sleeve for dressing and moving. The sleeve may be constructed with or without an underarm seam and the crisscross may be lapped toward the front or the back of the sleeve. A pattern for the petal sleeve may be developed from the basic set-in sleeve pattern.

To make a petal sleeve pattern

1. Fold the sleeve pattern into quarters.

2. Sketch in desired style line from front quarter.

3. Fold sleeve on center and trace style line to back of sleeve. Reverse the sleeve and trace in the remainder of the style line.

4. For a sleeve with underarm seam, trace off each section and indicate the grainline.

For a sleeve without an underarm seam, establish a grainline to represent the underarm seam. Trace the petal sleeve by placing the grainline at the front underarm seam and tracing front section. Repeat for back as illustrated.

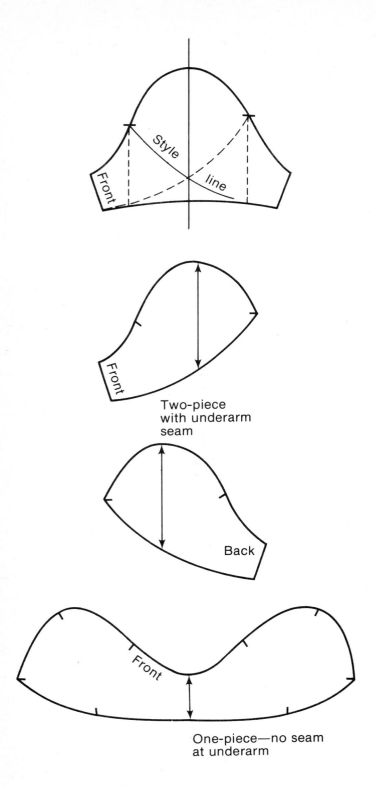

Style line

Front

Front

Two-piece
with underarm
seam

Back

Front

One-piece—no seam
at underarm

3. Jackets and coats

Jacket with hem raised at the back

A person who must sit down at all times finds it uncomfortable to sit on uneven folds and thicknesses of fabric. The excess length of a jacket may be eliminated by shortening the jacket in the seat area but retaining the original length at the sides and front.

Materials:
one suit jacket

Instructions:
Shortened back panel
1. Open back panel seams in jacket to just above the chair seat when a person is sitting down.

2. Hem the back panel of the jacket at this level and retain the original side and front hem.

Zippered suit jacket

Curved back hem

1. Shape jacket back from side seams to center back to form a smooth curve so the jacket back is just above the chair when the person is seated.

2. Hem curved edge.

A suit jacket may be altered to aid a person with restricted arm movement, by inserting zippers in the front sleeve and side front seam. Instructions overleaf.

Materials:
suit jacket
25 cm (10 in) zipper
40 cm (16 in) separating zipper or a zipper
the length of the arm seam
70 cm (28 in) of 2 cm (¾ in) twill tape
2.5 cm (1 in) Velcro

Instructions:
1. Remove stitching in side front seam from pocket to underarm, in front sleeve seam from wrist to underarm, and in armhole between these two seams for jacket and lining.

2. Stitch twill tape to front seam allowances to create a larger seam allowance for zipper insertion.

3. Insert conventional zipper from pocket to underarm. A lapped application is the least conspicuous method.

4. Insert separating zipper in sleeve seam, again using a lapped application.

5. Stitch Velcro to underarm opening between the two zippers.

6. Handstitch lining to edges of zipper tape.

Note: If the jacket used does not have a side panel, use two separating zippers: one to extend the length of the arm seam, the other the length of the side seam.

Jacket with top of sleeve zipper

For a person who has limited use of an arm, dressing may be facilitated by inserting a zipper in the garment sleeve from the sleeve cap to the wrist, or from neckline continuing through sleeve cap to the wrist if a longer opening is required. It could be done more easily on a jacket with a raglan or kimono sleeve.

Materials:
jacket, or fabric and notions for a jacket
separating zipper of suitable length
strip of knit fabric slightly longer than the zipper to be used and 8 cm (3 in) wide

Instructions:
Hand-made jacket

1. Modify the sleeve pattern by slashing it from the dot at the top of the shoulder along the straight-of-goods to the wrist.

2. Construct the jacket, leaving open the underarm seam of the sleeve, the shoulder seam, and the top of the sleeve along slashed line. Machine baste leaving underarm seam open to facilitate sewing in the zipper.

3. Center teeth of separating zipper under basted seam and top-stitch 6 mm (¼ in) on either side of the seam. Remove basting.

4. A fabric inset will help protect the skin from the abrasive action of the zipper. Fold the strip of fabric lengthwise, right sides together, and stitch ends. Trim and turn.

5. Stitch raw edge of inset to edge of back seam allowance so that the inset extends forward between the zipper and the body.

Jacket with center back zipper and center front button closing

A separating zipper at the center back of the jacket makes it easier to dress a person with limited ability to move.

Purchased jacket

(This assumes there is sufficient ease in the sleeve to allow zipper insertion.)

1. Remove stitching in the shoulder seam and slash sleeve as in Step 1 above.

2. Press 6 mm (¼ in) seam allowance under along opening.

3. Baste the separating zipper into the open seam leaving the zipper teeth exposed. Use a zipper foot to stitch 1.5 mm (¹⁄₁₆ in) from the zipper teeth along each side.

4. A fabric inset is needed to protect the body from the abrasive action of the zipper. Follow above procedure for inset, Step 4, stitching edge of inset to zipper tape.

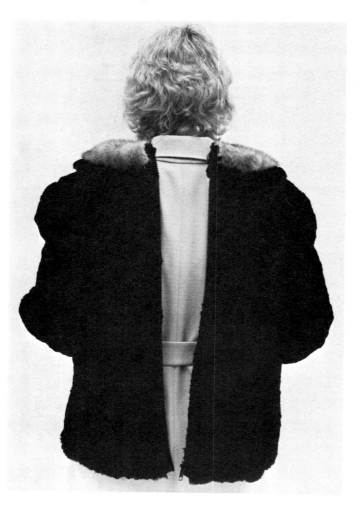

Materials:
one jacket, fabric or fur
separating zipper the length of the center
back of the coat
two large hooks and eyes
twill braid, twice the length of the zipper
fabric 8 cm (3 in) wide and the length of the
zipper

Instructions:
1. Split the jacket down center back.

2. Sew tape on both sides of the fabric (right side of fabric and tape together so that when the tape is folded to the inside the raw edges of the fabric are enclosed and a lip of the tape is exposed on the right side).

3. Hand stitch the tape to the inside of the fabric so the tape lies flat.

4. Stitch the zipper in place, from the lower edge to the neckline, by top stitching on the exposed tape.

5. Invisibly stitch the raw edges of upper and under collar together and sew hooks and eyes in place under collar so that the collar lies smoothly in place.

6. Hand stitch the lining in place so that the raw edges of lining, garment, and zipper are enclosed.

7. A fabric inset is necessary to prevent clothing from catching in the zipper teeth. Cut a piece of fabric the length of the zipper and 8 cm (3 in) wide. Fold the piece in half, right sides together and stitch the ends. Turn inset right side out and place underneath zipper tape. Topstitch in place on first line of stitching.

Note: If the jacket is for a person in a wheelchair, the jacket should come only to seat level so the person is not sitting on many layers of fabric. The jacket should be shortened accordingly. Inserting the zipper upside down would increase the comfort of the chair-bound and facilitate dressing by an assistant.

Kangaroo jacket

A sling may be built into a jacket for a person with an injured arm by adding a kangaroo pouch fastened by Velcro.

Materials:
pattern for loose fitted jacket with dropped shoulders
material as required
separating zipper the length of side and sleeve seam
30 cm (12 in) Velcro
0.30 m (⅓ yd) fabric for pouch

Instructions:
1. Compare size of armhole and sleeve to the cast or bandage on the arm. Cut the pattern as needed to supply ample room for the cast.

2. Insert a separating zipper into the side seam to extend from the hem of the jacket to the hem of the sleeve.

3. Cut one pouch from the accompanying pattern.

4. Turn under edges of pouch 1 cm (⅜ in) and topstitch.

5. Sew pouch to jacket in a location suitable for the sling along seamline ABCD.

6. Stitch Velcro onto right side of pouch to extend from E to F.

7. Fold pouch along fold line and apply Velcro to jacket in the appropriate location.

1 square = 1 cm (⅜ in)

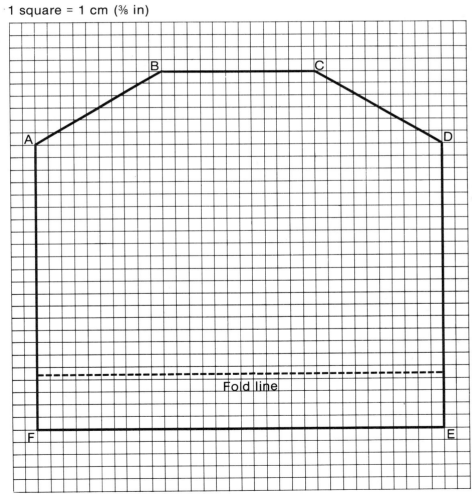

Fold line

Back action pleat

When constructing a garment it is possible to add a deep inverted pleat in the back of a blouse, dress, or jacket. This action pleat is particularly suitable for a person on crutches as it provides added room for movement.

In the jacket shown, the back is cut in Orlon pile. The extension for the pleat is cut from the same double knit as the sleeves and the band. An inverted pleat 7.5 cm (3 in) in width requires a total extension of 15 cm (6 in) or double the finished pleat, plus seam allowance.

Open side pile vest

This vest is warm, lightweight, and easy to put
on and remove. Any warm fabric could be
used, depending on the needs of the wearer.
Lining the vest will eliminate the facings
and make it easier to slip on over clothing.
Instructions overleaf.

Materials:
0.90 m (1 yd) fabric
0.80 m (⅞ yd) lining
2 large Velcro discs
regular pattern for top

Instructions:
1. Cut the back of fabric and lining from a regular pattern retaining the shoulder dart. Remove the underarm extensions as shown in the diagram below.

2. Cut the front of fabric and lining in two pieces with a deep V-neckline opening. Omit the bust darts and underarm extensions. Construct shoulder dart in the back.

3. Stitch front to back at shoulder seams of fabric and lining.

4. Stitch fabric and lining, right sides together, around neckline and armholes. Trim and pull right sides out through one shoulder seam. Understitch. Baste lining to fabric at waistline.

5. Cut fabric for waistbands, 13 cm (5 in) wide. The front waistband should be the same length as the two front pieces. The back waistband should extend 5 cm (2 in) on either side of the back bodice.

6. Stitch separate waistbands to bodice front and back.

7. Attach Velcro to waistband at side openings.

4. Dresses and aprons

Dress with side front opening

A seated person or a person with limited movement is dressed more easily if the garment opens flat. Velcro and/or a zipper added to the side front of a dress or blouse will facilitate dressing.

Materials:
commercial pattern for dress
fabric as required
45 cm (18 in) separating zipper
10 cm (4 in) Velcro
five buttons

Instructions:
If the pattern has a side front opening
1. Fasten the bodice with Velcro and stitch buttons on top of the opening.

2. Insert zipper from waistline to hem.

If the pattern does not have a side front opening
1. Establish new front opening line parallel to lengthwise grainline from a point on the shoulder seam 4 cm (1½ in) from the neckline (A).

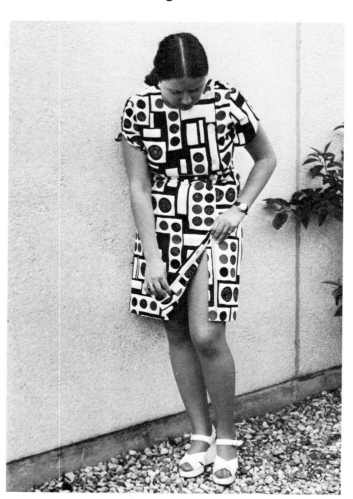

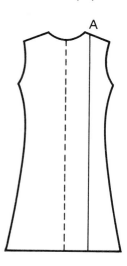

Dress with back opening

A garment which opens completely in the back simplifies the dressing of another person. A Velcro closure fastens the back bodice and waistline, and the skirt is lapped for ease in using bathroom facilities. Instructions overleaf.

2. Trace each pattern half. Add a 4 cm (1½ in) extension to the left side to meet the neckline. Add a 5 cm (2 in) facing to both pattern pieces.

3. Construct the dress following the basic directions in the pattern.

4. Attach Velcro to the bodice opening and stitch buttons to right side.

5. Insert separating zipper from waistline to hem so that bending is not necessary in order to fasten the zipper.

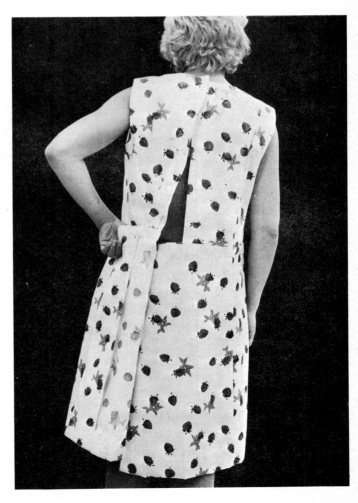

Materials:

commercial dress pattern
fabric as required plus an extra skirt length
40 cm (16 in) Velcro

Instructions:

1. If the pattern does not have a waistline seam, cut the back pattern at the waistline and center back. Add 16 mm (⅝ in) seam allowance to the skirt and bodice.

2. Add a 10 cm (4 in) extension to the right skirt pattern at center back. Add 20 cm (8 in) to left skirt pattern at center back for extension and facing.

3. Add a 3.5 cm (1⅜ in) extension to left bodice at center back.

4. Construct dress as the pattern directs but leave center back seam open.

5. Turn right bodice and skirt seam allowances under 16 mm (⅝ in) and topstitch edge.

6. Fold left bodice facing to wrong side and topstitch.

7. Place right sides of left skirt and facing together, and stitch at waistline from fold to center back. Grade and understitch seam. Press facing to the wrong side.

8. Attach Velcro to back bodice opening and extension at waistline.

9. Hem the dress.

Side opening dress
with released waistline seam

A garment which opens out flat is much easier for a seated person or a person with limited arm dexterity to put on than one that must be pulled over the head. Arm movement is less restricted when reaching if the waistline seam is released at the side to allow the bodice to move with the shoulder.

Materials:
commercial pattern for sleeveless, collarless dress
fabric as required
1 separating zipper the length of the bodice
1 separating zipper the length of the skirt
5 cm (2 in) Velcro

Instructions:
1. Add a 7 cm (2¾ in) extension to waistline seam of back and front skirt pattern from waistline darts to side seams.

2. Stitch darts, left side seams, center back, and center front seams.

3. Finish the three edges of extensions.

4. Attach bodice front and bodice back to skirt between the waistline darts.

5. Press waistline seam allowances up and handstitch bodice seam allowance in place from waistline darts to side seams.

6. Stitch left shoulder seam.

7. Insert separating zippers in the right side, one extending from armhole to waistline, the other from waistline to hem.

8. Attach facing to neck and armhole, leaving right shoulder seam free.

9. Fasten right shoulder seam with Velcro.

Wrap-around skirt and vest

Wrap-around garments are easier to put on than ones that must be stepped into or pulled over the head. A skirt with fullness added as pleats or flare is desirable for ease of movement.

Materials:
commercial pattern for skirt and V-neck vest
fabric as required
43 cm (17 in) Velcro

Instructions:
Skirt
If pattern is wrap-around
1. Fasten at ends of waistband and overlap with Velcro.

If pattern is not wrap-around
1. Fold out all pleats in skirt front pattern.

2. Trace the second skirt front.

3. Cut fabric.

4. Stitch darts and pleats. Press.

5. Stitch original skirt front to right back and second skirt front to left back.

6. Finish side front edges.

7. Attach waistband.

8. The skirt should overlap to the left. Attach 2.5 cm (1 in) Velcro to each end of waistband so both the overlap and underlap portions are secure. Attach 18 cm (7 in) Velcro in a vertical position to the left side overlap to hold it in position.

9. Hem skirt.

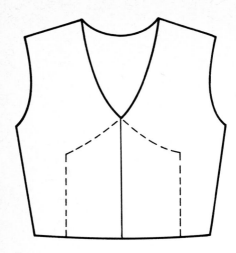

Vest

If wrap-around pattern is used
1. Fasten overlap with Velcro.

If pattern is not a wrap-around
1. Sketch new design line onto pattern (see dotted . . . line).

2. Trace this new pattern and cut fabric (each front will be identical).

3. Stitch darts and shoulder seams.

4. Finish neck edge and edge of overlaps.

5. Stitch side seams.

6. Attach armhole facing.

7. Hem vest.

8. Attach 10 cm (4 in) Velcro to each edge of overlap so the right side overlaps the left side.

The "big dress" currently popular in fashion allows lots of skirt and bodice room for movement, and conceals any necessary appliances. Loose-fitting garments are comfortable for sitting as well as standing. (See also page 73.)

Butterick pattern no. 4125

Adjusting commercial patterns for the handicapped

Many commercially available patterns may be easily adjusted to meet the needs of the handicapped. One example is the dress on this page which incorporates a variety of features already described in other sections.

Special features of this garment include the front zipper with the pull, the easy fastening adjustable belt, gathers rather than the more constricting bust dart, side pleats, an inverted back pleat and open underarm dolman sleeves for ease of movement, in-seam pockets concealed by the side pleats, and a slightly lowered neck seam for comfort. Flat seam construction helps eliminate skin irritation from raw fabric edges.

An example of a pattern which could easily be adapted to make a garment such as the one shown is Simplicity 9148.

Two-piece wrap-around skirt

The wrap-around skirt has a back opening for added comfort when the person is seated. A separate back panel may be tied in front to cover the back opening when the person wishes to move around.

Materials:
2.40 m (2⅝ yd) 115 cm (45 in) fabric
16 cm (6¼ in) Velcro
61 cm (24 in) 2.5 cm (1 in) elastic

Instructions:
For the main skirt
1. Cut a piece of fabric which is the full width of the fabric and the desired length of the skirt plus 7 cm (2½ in) hem allowance.

2. The selvedge edges may be used to form the back opening of the skirt. Gather the top of the skirt so that it is 8 cm (3 in) shorter than the waist measurement.

3. Cut a strip of fabric 18 cm (7 in) wide and the length of waist plus a 8 cm (3 in) extension for the waistband.

4. Stitch ends of waistband and extension.

5. Apply waistband to skirt top, matching end of waistband to back opening on one side and leaving a 15 cm (6 in) extension on other end.

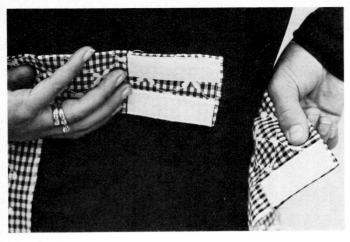

6. Attach Velcro to the waistband so the waistband is adjustable. Cut Velcro into two 8 cm (3 in) pieces. Stitch the two napped sections of Velcro to the waistband extension in horizontal positions. Use only one of the hook sections of Velcro and stitch it to the other waistband extension in a vertical position.

7. Hem lower edge of skirt.

For the back panel

1. Cut fabric the desired length of the skirt plus hem allowance, and the width of the fabric.

2. Fold selvedge edges under at front opening and hem.

3. Fold 4 cm (1½ in) under on upper edge of panel and stitch close to edge to form a casing.

4. Thread elastic through casing and secure at front edges.

5. For ties, cut two strips 10 cm (4 in) wide and 90 cm (36 in) long. Fold ties in half, lengthwise, right sides together, and stitch one end and side. Turn to right side. Turn under raw end and stitch ties to ends of elastic casing.

6. Hem back panel.

Skirt with partial back

The wrap-around skirt with partial back allows a person to dress while seated and prevents sitting on excess folds of fabric.

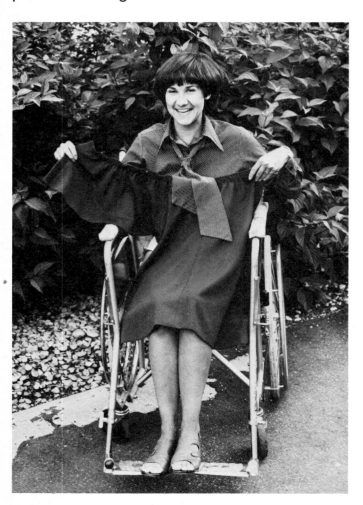

Materials:
one purchased skirt
25 cm (10 in) Velcro

or

60 cm (⅔ yd) fabric
2.5 cm (1 in) elastic, 8 cm (3 in) less than the circumference of waist
25 cm (10 in) Velcro

Instructions:
If altering a purchased skirt
1. Open left side seam from hem to waist.

2. Cut across skirt back to right side seam at a level just above the chair (plus hem allowance) when the person is seated.

3. Remove this lower skirt back section by opening the lower part of the right side seam.

4. The original side seam allowances of the skirt are too narrow to form the edges of a wrap-around skirt. From the unused back portion of the skirt, cut strips of fabric 4 cm (1½ in) wide to form a facing. Stitch the facing strips to the side seams. Trim and grade seam; understitch.

5. Hem skirt back.

6. Hand stitch edge of side seam facing to the skirt so it will lie flat.

7. Stitch Velcro to edge of flap and to the left skirt front to fasten the flap in place.

If constructing the A-line skirt

1. Cut the front as the pattern shows but extend the seam allowances to 4 cm (1½ in) to form a facing.

2. Shorten the back pattern piece to just above the chair when the person is seated (plus the hem).

3. Extend the left side back seam allowance to 2.5 cm (1 in).

4. Cut skirt back.

5. Stitch center front seam and center back seam.

6. Hem skirt back.

7. Stitch right side seams together.

8. Fold under 4 cm (1½ in) facing on side front seam and stitch in place by hand.

9. Stitch Velcro to left side of skirt front and skirt back, to hold skirt back and front in place.

10. Match edge of elastic to right side of fabric at top of waistline. Trim excess fabric. Turn elastic to wrong side so that it does not show from the right side. Stitch along the upper and lower edges of the elastic.

11. Hem skirt front.

Dress with skirt back removed

A person sitting in a wheelchair may not be able to lift herself off the chair. To eliminate the need to rise for dressing, the lower skirt back may be removed from a dress with a front opening. The garment can then be placed around the person and fastened without difficulty. The absence of the lower skirt back also means that the person is not sitting on uncomfortable folds of fabric. This dress would be suitable for an incontinent condition as only the underclothes would need to be changed.

Clip-on apron

Clip-on plastic waistbands are available in large department stores. The band is threaded through a casing at the top of the apron and is easily removed to launder the apron.

Materials:
clip-on plastic waistband
0.60 m (⅔ yd) of 90 cm (36 in) fabric

Instructions:
1. Use full width of fabric so that selvedges form the edges of the apron.

2. Fold upper raw edge under 6 mm (¼ in) and then 4 cm (1½ in). Topstitch close to lower folded edge and 2 cm (⅞ in) away from first line to form a casing.

3. Hem to the desired length.

4. Thread plastic band through casing.

Bias cut apron

A woven fabric which is cut on the bias conforms more closely to the body shape. An apron which is cut on the bias would fit more smoothly and be less likely to get in the way. A large pocket gathered at the top with elastic helps prevent articles from spilling out of the pocket. Rather than the usual back tie closing, which may be difficult for a person with limited finger dexterity, the apron has a Velcro closure at the more easily accessible side position.

Full apron

Aprons which slip over the head can easily be put on by a person with limited movement. Closures may be eliminated by the use of straps which cross over in the back and are fastened to the shoulder and side of the apron's bodice. A chair-bound person may find side tie closures easier to manage than straps.

McCalls pattern no. 3845

Half apron with pocket and towel

The apron shown features a deep pocket which hangs loose from the waistband. The advantage of this type of pocket is that it will hang down by the side when the person sits, and thus the contents are not so apt to fall out. The detachable hand towel is particularly useful in the kitchen. The waistband may be fastened with Velcro or finished with ties, depending on the capabilities of the wearer.

5. Nightwear

One-piece wrapped gown

This garment may be worn as a nightgown or a lounging dress. It opens out flat and ties to adjust to body size. Waistline ties fasten the panels in the front and back. There are no seams to rub against the skin, and the back panel can be pulled aside, thus making it more comfortable when sitting.

Materials:
2.3 m (2½ yd) of 90 cm (36 in) or 115 cm (45 in) wide fabric
9.2 m (10 yd) single-fold bias tape

Instructions:
1. Bind the neckline opening of the gown.

2. Stitch bias tape to edge AB and EF.

3. Attach tape to edge CD for sleeves.

4. Bind edges along BC and DE, leaving sufficient tape at B and E to tie around the waist.

5. To enclose the raw edges of bias tape, make a small dart at points C and D.

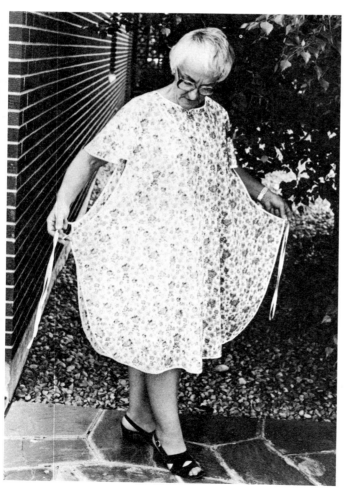

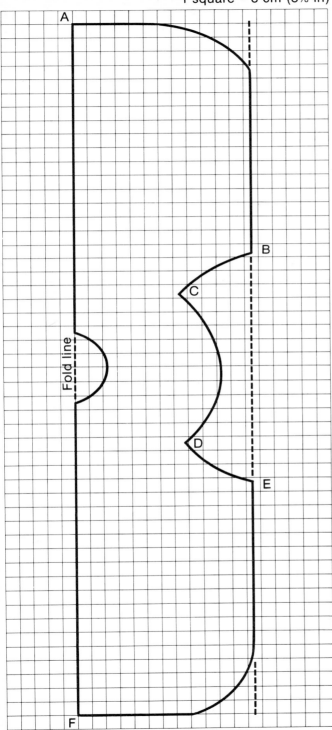

1 square = 8 cm (3⅛ in)

A

B

C

Fold line

D

E

F

Two-piece wrapped gown

This garment may be worn as a dress or as loungewear. It consists of two separate identical pieces, a right half and a left half. The ties at each underarm provide adjustment to body size. There is only one seam at the side of each panel. The cap sleeves and neckline are bound with soft bias binding. Instructions overleaf.

109

Materials:

2.3 m (2½ yd) of 90 cm (36 in) fabric
4.6 m (5 yd) single-fold bias tape
2 belt rings 2.5 cm (1 in) diameter

Instructions:

1. Stitch bias binding to the neckline opening of the gown, leaving 25 cm (10 in) beyond each A and B for ties.

2. Stitch bias tape to the armhole edge, from C to D.

3. Bind edges along GA and BH.

4. Sew underarm seam joining CF and DE.

5. Hem lower edge of garment GFEH.

6. Fold belt along foldline, stitch outer edge along length and pointed end.

7. Turn belt right side out, finish other end.

8. Lap fabric at the square end of belt placing rings between fabric thicknesses. Stitch.

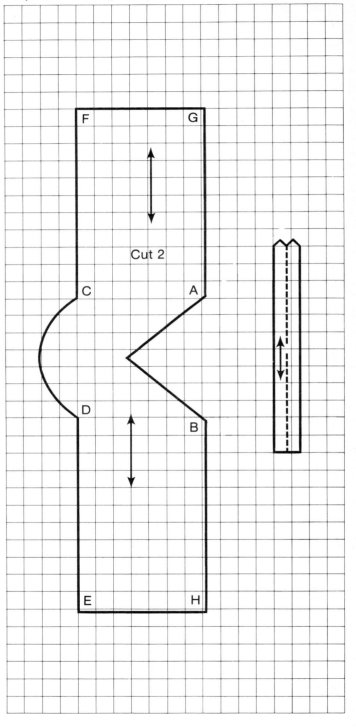

1 square = 8 cm (3⅛ in)

Cut 2

Wrap-around
three armhole garment

The principle of a three armhole garment can be used for dresses, aprons, or nighties. This garment can be wrapped at back or front. It has no buttons or zippers, hence it is easier to handle by a person with restricted finger movements and is also easier to launder. It also has the advantage of being easy to slip on and off and of concealing irregularities in body shape. The neckline can be high or scooped, depending on individual likes as well as on intended use of garment.

The finished length of this garment at center front is 89 cm (35 in). It can be lengthened or shortened by slashing and adding or folding the pattern at the line indicated. Place the pattern on the lengthwise fold of fabric.

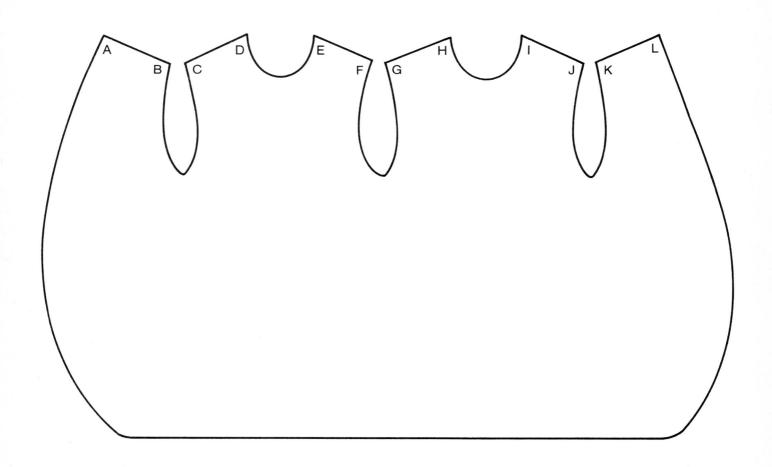

Join the shoulder seams AB and CD, EF and
GH, IJ and KL with French seams to conceal
cut edges or with plain seams and overcast
seam allowances. Try the garment on to
check the fit at the neckline and armholes. All
edges are then bound with bias tape. Add
a pocket or two where it seems most
comfortable to have them.

1 square = 3.7 cm (1½ in)

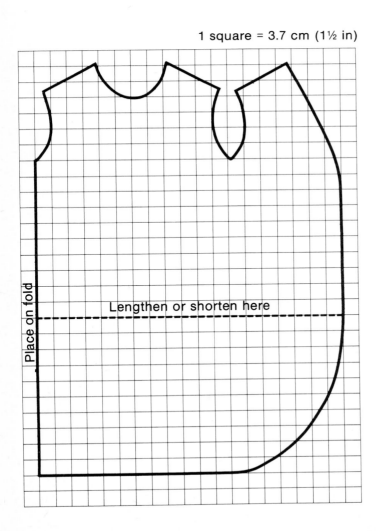

Place on fold

Lengthen or shorten here

Nightgown
with a lapped back
and front zipper

A nightgown with a lapped back opening simplifies the use of bathroom facilities. This technique is suitable for a wide variety of garments such as housecoats and dresses. The long front zipper makes it easy for a person to dress from a sitting position.

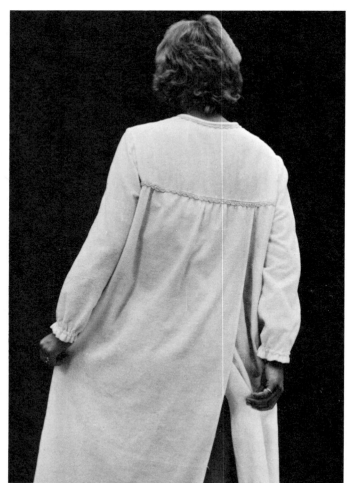

Nightgown with cross-over bodice

Materials:
commercial pattern with front opening and yoke or waistline seam
sufficient fabric for pattern and a 20 cm (8 in) extension to each side of center back

Instructions:
1. Add a 20 cm (8 in) extension to each side of center back pattern.

2. Turn under 6 mm (¼ in) on lengthwise edge of back panel, and stitch. Turn under a further 5 cm (2 in) on each lengthwise edge of back panel and press.

3. Lap back panels so that the original center backs are aligned.

4. Baste the back panels together at waist or yoke seamline.

5. Construct garment as directed in the pattern.

Note: A similar lap can be created in the front of the nightgown.

A nightgown with a bias cross-over bodice and kimono sleeves eliminates the possibility of binding at the neckline and armholes. The gown slips easily over the head without the need for a fastening. The front and back lapped skirt facilitates bathroom functions. Instructions overleaf.

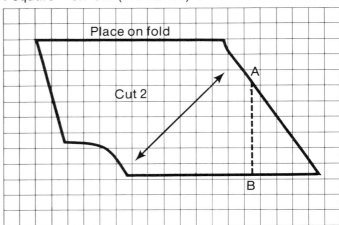

1 square = 3.7 cm (1½ inches)

Place on fold

Cut 2

A

B

Materials:

2.80 m (3 yd) of 90 cm (36 in) fabric
2.60 m (2⅞ yd) bias tape
13 mm (½ in) elastic to fit snugly under bust

Instructions:

1. Cut two of the bodice pattern and two pieces of fabric 90 cm (36 in) wide and the length desired for the gown.

2. Stitch underarm seams of bodice sections. Use bias tape to bind neckline edges and sleeve hems.

3. Match the two bodice sections at center front and center back (line AB) and baste together at waistline seam.

4. Hem four lapped edges and lower edges of skirt pieces.

5. Match skirt sections to bodice at waistline seam, so that ends of skirt lap match ends of cross-over on bodice. Ease skirt to fit. Stitch bodice to skirt.

6. Join ends of elastic in a circle. Divide circle in quarters and match quarter points to side seams, center front, and center back of gown. Stitch elastic to wrong side of gown, centering over waistline seam.

Gown with envelope neckline

This gown has no closures, and yet fits closely and comfortably. The envelope neckline (shown on page 59) which laps at the shoulder slips easily over the head. Petal sleeves (shown on page 74) allow room for movement. The skirt laps in back and front (shown on page 114), simplifying the use of bathroom facilities.

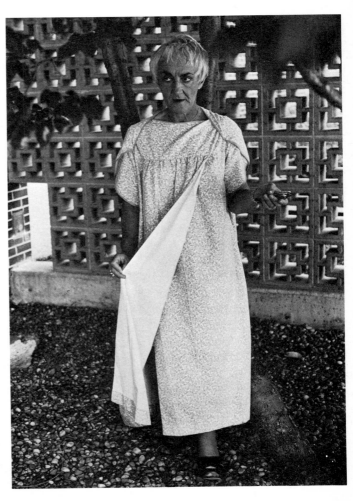

Front closing nightgown

This nightgown can be made by altering an ordinary commercial pattern so that the garment has a full length opening and an overlap of approximately 15 cm (6 in) to 20 cm (8 in). The one illustrated fastens with two pieces of Velcro. Snaps could also be used. It is ideal for persons whose arm movements are restricted and who do not have the finger dexterity necessary to fasten buttons or ties. It is also ideal for nursing mothers since it allows for maximum coverage while nursing the infant.

Materials:
commercial pattern for nightgown
fabric required by pattern plus enough to cut the front pieces 15 cm (6 in) wider.

Instructions:
1. Add a 15 cm (6 in) extension to the skirt at center front. This includes a 5 cm (2 in) facing.

2. Redraw the front neckline curve to extend 10 cm (4 in) beyond center front, so that it matches the skirt overlap. Cut a facing to match.

3. Sew the gown as the pattern directs, incorporating the overlapped front opening.

4. Sew Velcro or snaps at the waistline to fasten the gown.

Nightwear
opened at center back

This is a good gift for a person going to the hospital for surgery or for an elderly person confined to bed. A center back opening and an overlap of one inch has been added to a conventional nightgown pattern. The gown is closed by Velcro but it could have ties instead. Such a nightgown can be made of any fabric. This one is made from a cotton and polyester knit with a dainty flower pattern.

This nightgown can be easily put on and taken off. When sitting up the wearer does not need to close the lower part; hence if she is incontinent, the nightie does not necessarily get soiled.

Commercially made nightgowns or pyjama tops can be slashed down center back. Each side can be faced with a matching fabric and pieces of Velcro sewn to close the opening.

Men's pyjamas

Shown is a man's pyjama top with center
back opening, and pyjama bottoms with long
side placket openings. The front of the
pyjama bottoms is held up with waistline ties
while the drop seat fastens at the waistline
with Velcro.

Wrap-around
men's pyjama top

Men's pyjama bottoms

If tying is easier than manipulating other closures, this pyjama top may prove popular. It is cut with roomy, kimono sleeves, lapped over front, and has a tie belt.

These pants feature a back seat inset which provides room when the person sits. This cut should prove to be comfortable, roomy, and free from binding for the person who sits much of the time.

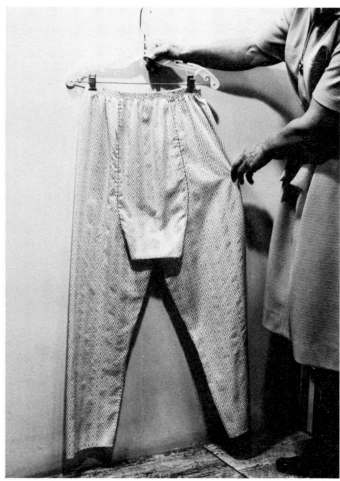

6. Underwear

Panties or undershorts with side opening

Panties or undershorts may be opened on one side (not on side seam) and fastened with Velcro or with hooks and eyes. This will facilitate dressing when a leg brace or high leg cast is worn.

Materials:
panties or undershorts
Velcro to fit side length of garment
tricot or soft fabric to form underlap

Instructions:
1. Cut through side front of panties or side front of undershorts.

2. Stitch a 7 cm (2¾ in) long extension of double fabric to the side seam of the panties or shorts. Stitch one strip of Velcro on top of this seam so that right side of Velcro is on right side of extension.

3. Turn front edge under and stitch. Attach Velcro along front edge so that right side of Velcro is on wrong side of side front opening.

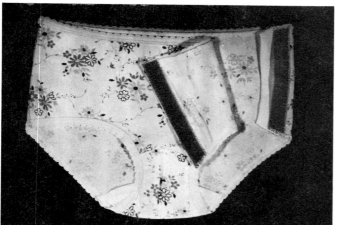

Men's or women's underpants

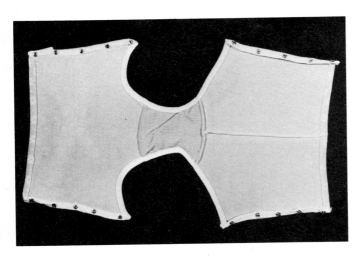

Materials:
pair of women's underpants
tape or strips of fabric to finish the raw edges
and create a small lap on each side
snaps or Velcro

Instructions:
1. Remove stitching at side seams.

2. Finish the raw edges and create a lap by sewing strips of fabric or cloth tape to the sides.

3. Attach snaps or Velcro.

Underpants which open flat aid in dressing. Although the photographs show only adaptations to women's underpants, the same alterations can be done for men's undershorts.

Women's underpants with front fastened crotch

Underpants with a crotch that opens in front make it easier to change the protective pads used by an incontinent person.

Materials:
a pair of underpants
15 cm (6 in) cloth tape
snaps

Instructions:
1. Cut front crotch seam open.

2. Finish the raw edges with cloth tape, creating a small lap in the process.

3. Attach snaps for fastening.

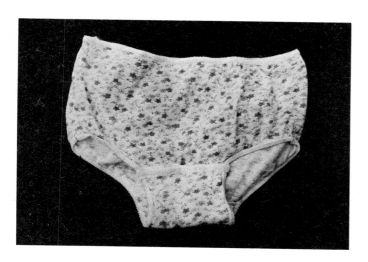

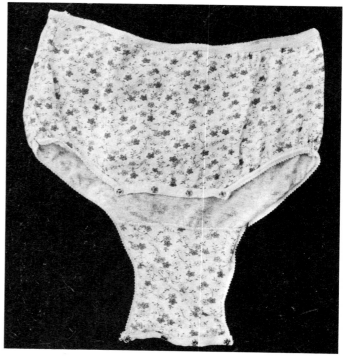

Undershorts or panties with front flap

Undershorts or panties which open out flat and fasten with a front flap make it easier to dress a person who needs assistance in dressing. The same garment may be worn with protective padding for incontinence.

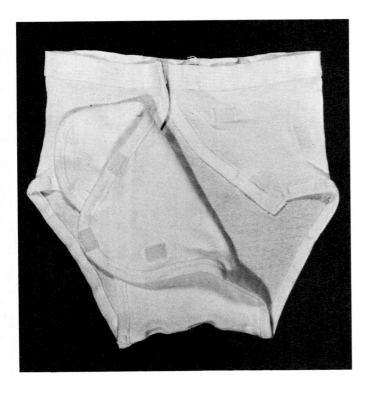

Materials:
undershorts or panties
13 cm (5 in) Velcro
0.20 m (¼ yd) knit fabric

Instructions:
1. Slash from center front at waistline, through elastic and diagonally to leg edge at front crotch seam on each side of garment. Slash through the back crotch seam to remove the entire crotch gusset.

2. Cut a continuous front flap and crotch gusset of double thickness from the knit fabric. The flap should be approximately 18 cm (7 in) wide from the waistline to the leg seam. Extend the flap into the crotch gusset using the original gusset as a pattern.

3. Stitch the new gusset to the back crotch seam.

4. Cut 2.5 cm (1 in) strips of knit fabric on the crosswise grain and bind all raw edges.

5. Attach Velcro at waist and on the four corners of the front flap to hold the flap in place.

Undershorts or panties with front flap and tape loop

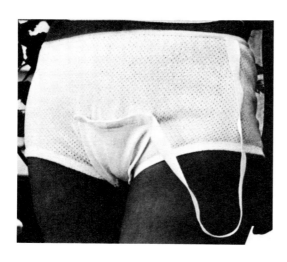

When a person has difficulty in lowering undergarments to use bathroom facilities, the addition of a front flap opening and tape loop may be beneficial. The tape loop allows the flap to be manipulated with the hand or foot.

Materials:
pair of men's undershorts or women's panties
13 x 23 cm (5 x 9 in) of soft matching knit fabric
87 cm (34 in) twill tape
8 cm (3¼ in) Velcro

Instructions:
1. Cut panties or shorts apart on front crotch seam. Bind raw edge of body part with twill tape.

2. With right sides together, fold knit fabric in half, and stitch to form a piece 15 x 11 cm (5 x 4½ in). Stitch across one end. Trim corners. Turn right side out.

3. Stitch the open end of the tube of fabric to raw edge of the crotch piece. Zig-zag or overcast raw edges.

4. Attach twill tape to upper left hand corner of added flap. Stitch the other end of the tape to the waist, at the side seam. This forms the tape loop.

5. Attach Velcro to the underside of the flap piece and to the body of the panties or shorts to hold the flap in position.

Men's undershorts

An opening at the waist of undershorts, fastened by Velcro, increases the waist circumference for ease of dressing and use of bathroom facilities.

Materials:
undershorts
10 cm (4 in) Velcro
10 cm (4 in) of elastic the same width as that on the shorts

Instructions:
1. Remove the stitches holding the double layer of crotch front fabric to the elastic at the waist.

2. Cut the elastic at the left side of the double layer.

3. Re-sew under-panel to the elastic.

4. Stitch the new piece of elastic to the top panel and to the cut edge of the original elastic.

5. Stitch the Velcro to the elastic between the two layers.

Undershorts or panties with tape loop

It is sometimes difficult for a person to bend down to remove clothing such as undergarments. A twill tape loop may be added so that shorts or panties may be removed by pulling on the loop with a foot. A person with limited or no use of arms may find this a useful modification.

Materials:
1 pair undershorts or panties
twill tape

Instructions:
1. Stitch one end of the twill tape to the left leg band in the center of the left front panel.

2. Position the tape so that a loop of 12 cm (5 in) long is left hanging, and secure the other end of the tape to the waistband.

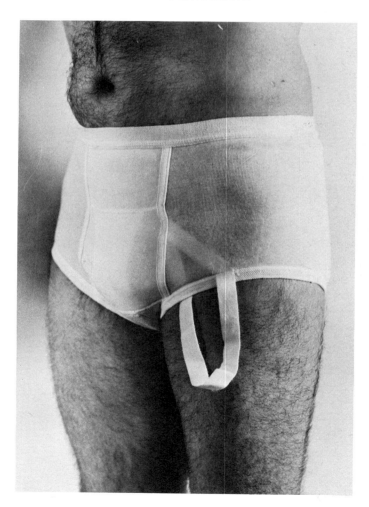

130

Garter belt with front closure

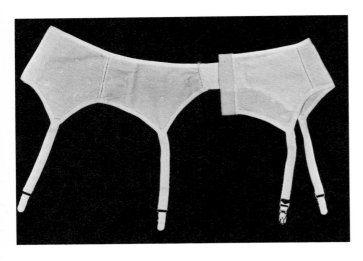

Garter belts with hook closures in the back are difficult to fasten. The problem can be alleviated by moving the closure to a front position.

Materials:
13 cm (5 in) Velcro
13 cm (5 in) twill tape [2.5 cm (1 in) wide] garter belt

Instructions:
1. Remove hooks and eyes at back of garment.

2. Lap edge of garment and stitch securely together.

3. Slash garment down center front.

4. Turn cut edge under 3 mm (⅛ in) and stitch in place.

5. Attach twill tape to form a 2.5 cm (1 in) extension on one side of front opening.

6. Attach Velcro to center front opening of belt so that original circumference is not changed.

Wrap-around garter belt

Materials:
twill tape 2.5 cm (1 in) wide
23 cm (9 in) of Velcro
7 large skirt hooks and eyes
1 wrap-around garter belt
3 bathing suit hooks

Instructions:
1. Remove hooks and eyes and replace them with seven large skirt hooks and eyes.

2. Attach three bathing suit hooks to the left back-side panel, one near the waist, one near the bottom, and one in the center of the panel.

3. Stitch twill tape to garter belt right front panel in a position corresponding to the bathing suit hooks.

4. Thread the twill tape through the corresponding bathing suit hook. Pull the tape back to the front to determine the placement of the Velcro on the tapes so the garter belt can be held in place to make fastening of the hooks easier.

5. Attach 8 cm (3 in) of Velcro to the ends of each tape.

It is awkward to hold the two sides of a wide garter belt together while the small hooks are fastened. Adjustable straps can be added to hold the garment temporarily in place while the hooks are fastened. The small hooks can be replaced by larger ones.

Girdles with zippers added

Zippers may be added to both regular and panty girdles to increase the circumference and make the garment easier to put on.

Materials:

regular girdle
two 22 cm (9 in) zippers
two strips knit fabric, 10 x 26 cm (4 x 10¼ in)

panty girdle
three 18 cm (7 in) zippers
three strips knit fabric, 10 x 21 cm (4 x 8¼ in)

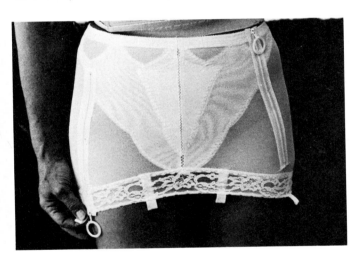

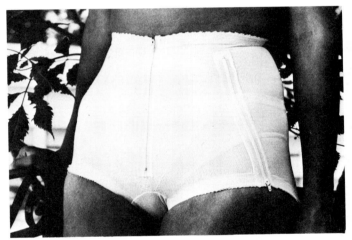

Instructions:

Two zippers should be added: one beginning at the waist and extending towards the leg; the other beginning at the leg and extending towards the waist. The zippers should be placed approximately in the center of each front panel.

Three zippers can be added: one at center front beginning at the waist and extending downward; the second and third beginning at the leg and extending towards the waist. These two zippers should be placed approximately in the center of each front panel.

Bra with front closure

An ordinary bra may be modified to close at the front with Velcro for ease of dressing, for a person who cannot fasten back closures.

Materials:
bra
Velcro
15 cm (6 in) lace or other suitable soft fabric
13 cm (5 in) of 2.5 cm (1 in) lingerie elastic

Instructions:
1. Remove back hooks and replace with 2.5 cm (1 in) elastic.

2. Cut bra at center front and bind raw edges with suitable fabric.

3. Attach Velcro closure. Protect skin from Velcro with a strip of fabric.

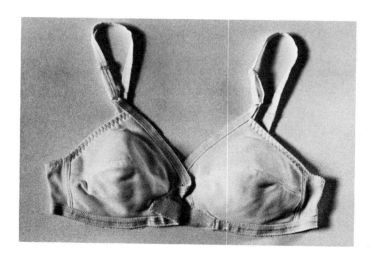

To insert the zippers:
1. Place zipper as indicated in A or B, folding upper edge under to match edge of girdle.

2. Using small stitches, topstitch into place along tape edges.

3. Cut away fabric from underneath zipper teeth.

4. An inset is needed to protect the body from the abrasive action of the zipper. Fold strip of fabric, right sides together, and stitch across the upper end. Trim and turn.

5. Baste inset underneath zipper, matching edge to zipper tape and girdle edge. Topstitch through zipper and inset along one edge of zipper tape and lower edge, to hold the inset smoothly in place.

Bra with adapted front closure

A bra with front closure may be adapted to make dressing easier by replacing small hooks with larger ones. A front strap allows the bra edges to be held together, thus making it possible to close the hooks if the wearer has only the use of one hand, or if finger movements are greatly impaired.

Materials:
bra with front closure
five skirt hooks
70 cm (28 in) of 2 cm (¾ in) twill tape
5 cm (2 in) Velcro
large bra fastener

Instructions:
1. Remove regular hooks and eyes from bra and remove stitching between front seam and facing.

2. Fasten skirt hooks to wrong side of front opening. Replace facing so that flat part of hook is covered, and slipstitch seam.

3. Construct larger thread eyes on opposite side of bra.

4. Stitch twill tape to front of bra under thread eyes, forming an extension to protect the body from the large hooks.

5. Fasten Velcro to each end of a 50 cm (20 in) piece of twill tape. Stitch one end to underarm of bra. Stitch large bra fastener to opposite side of bra. Thread other end of twill tape through the bra fastener. The twill tape can then form a loop which can be used to hold the bra together while the hooks are being fastened.

Slip with front zipper

A lightweight nylon or polyester zipper can be added to the front of a slip for easier dressing.

Materials:

full-length slip
40 cm (16 in) featherweight zipper
90 cm (1 yd) lace trim

Instructions:

1. Center zipper on center front line. Topstitch zipper to fabric around edges of zipper tape.

2. Trim fabric underneath zipper to edge of stitching.

3. Topstitch lace trim to cover edge of zipper tape.

Slip with bra cups attached

Materials:
slip with snug fitting seam under the bust and a front opening (See slip with front zipper)
bra or bra cups

Instructions:
1. If a bra is used, cut the cups out.

2. Position cups into slip to fit the bust.

3. Handstitch the cups to the slip.

It is more convenient for a person with restricted arm movement to put on a combined bra and slip than two separate garments. Ready-made bra slips are available, or bra cups may be sewn into a slip.

Slip with detachable bra

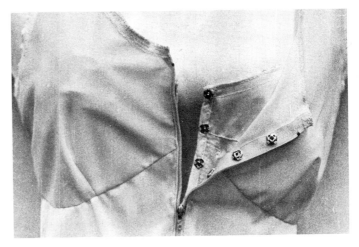

A bra may be snapped to a slip so that one closure fastens both garments. This would make it easier to dress oneself or someone else. The snaps allow undergarments to be interchanged. Instructions overleaf.

Materials:

full length slip with front opening (See slip
with front zipper)
bra
10 snaps
20 cm (8 in) lace or seam binding

Instructions:

1. Cut bra through center front.

2. Bind raw edges with bias tape.

3. Position bra into slip to fit the bust and
apply four snaps on each side of center front
to attach bra to slip.

4. Prepare a lace loop to attach to the
shoulder seams of the slip to hold the bra and
slip straps together. Cut a piece of lace the
length of the shoulder seam plus seam
allowances. Stitch the lace to one end of the
shoulder seam and fasten the other with
a snap.

5. Stitch a lace loop at center back to hold the
back of the bra in place. Cut a piece of lace
approximately 4 cm (1⅝ in) longer than the
width of the bra at center back. Turn under
edges of lace and stitch both ends to the
slip.

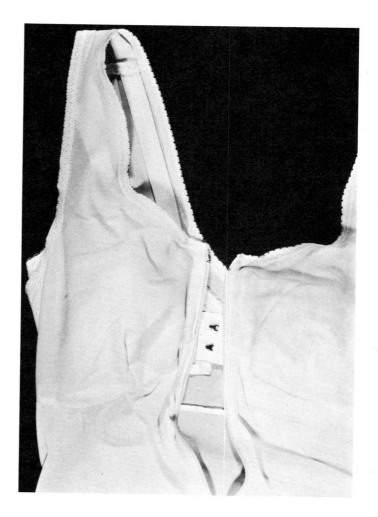

Wrap-around half slip

A wrap-around slip can be opened flat for easier dressing. It fastens with Velcro and can be worn with the lap in the front or the back.

Materials:
lingerie tricot, the desired length of the slip
lingerie elastic, waist measurement plus
10 cm (4 in)
Velcro
lace trim

Instructions:
1. Cut a rectangle of fabric of the dimensions shown in diagram.

2. Sew a piece of elastic to the top of the rectangle. Make the elastic of a length such that it fits comfortably around the waist, approximately 8–10 cm (3–4 in) less than the waist measurement, and allows for a 15–20 cm (6–8 in) lap.

3. Raw edges of the fabric may be finished with decorative lace or with a narrow hem.

4. Attach small pieces of Velcro to fasten both ends of the lap securely in place.

Hip measurement 46 cm (18⅛ in)
(to allow for ease and an overlap)

Desired length
of slip plus
hem allowance
if required

7. Children's wear

Jumper with Velcro shoulder fasteners

Ruffled jumper

Velcro discs at the shoulders of this child's jumper make dressing a simple task. To remove the garment, simply release the fasteners at the shoulders.

The ruffled shoulder line of this jumper could be a concealing feature for back and shoulder deformities. The open armholes promote ease of dressing and movement.

Shirt with stretch inserts in raglan sleeves

A person using a wheelchair or crutches needs more room in the sleeve for movement than can be provided by a woven fabric. Inserting strips of knit fabric in the raglan sleeve seam will give the necessary ease.

Materials:
shirt with raglan sleeves
20 cm (¼ yd) stretchy knit fabric

Instructions:
1. Cut four strips of knit fabric, 5 cm (2 in) wide and the length of the raglan seam long.

2. Remove collar or facing from neckline.

3. Separate sleeve from bodice by removing the stitching in the raglan sleeve seam.

4. Remove stitching in sleeve and side seam for 8 cm (3 in) at underarm.

5. Mark on the garment a new seamline 2.5 cm (1 in) on either side of the original raglan sleeve seam. Cut on these lines.

6. With right sides together, stitch inset and garment together using a 5 mm (¼ in) seam allowance.

7. Join underarm seams again.

8. Replace collar or facing.

T-shirt with large nylon zipper

T-shirts may be made easier to put on and take off by the addition of large nylon zippers with easily grasped zipper pulls. These zippers can be in matching or contrasting colors to add interest to the garment. This may help a child learn to dress himself by eliminating the need to master small fastenings.

T-shirt with separating zipper in side seam and sleeve

For a person whose arm movements are limited, dressing may be facilitated by inserting a separating zipper in the side and sleeve seams of a T-shirt.

144

Materials:

T-shirt or pattern, fabric, and notions for
T-shirt
40 cm (16 in) separating zipper or one of
suitable length
strip of knit fabric 44 x 8 cm (17¼ x 3 in)

Instructions:
Hand-made T-shirt

1. Construct the T-shirt, leaving open one
side seam from sleeve band to hem. Machine
baste this seam closed.

2. Center teeth of separating zipper under
basted seam and topstitch 6 mm (¼ in) on
either side of the seam. Remove basting.

3. A fabric inset is needed to protect the skin
from the abrasive action of the zipper. Fold
the strip of fabric lengthwise, right sides
together, and stitch ends. Trim and turn.

4. Stitch raw edge of inset to edge of back
seam allowance so that the inset extends
forward between the zipper and the body.

Purchased T-shirt

1. Remove stitching in one side and sleeve
seam and clip through sleeve band.

2. Press 6 mm (¼ in) seam allowance under
along opening.

3. Baste the separating zipper into the open
seam leaving the zipper teeth exposed. Use a
zipper foot to stitch 1.5 mm (1/16 in) from
the zipper teeth along each side.

4. A fabric inset is needed to protect the body
from the abrasive action of the zipper. Follow
above procedure for inset (Step 4), stitching
edge of inset to zipper tape.

T-shirt with shoulder opening

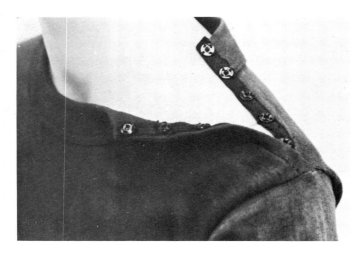

A larger opening to allow a T-shirt to be pulled over a child's head may be achieved by applying snap fasteners to the shoulder seam.

Materials:
T-shirt
20 cm (8 in) of 2 cm (¾ in) twill tape
five snap fasteners

Instructions:
1. Remove stitching in left shoulder seam to 1 cm (⅜ in) from sleeve cap. Secure end of stitching.

2. Enclose raw edges of both seam allowances with twill tape, turning under ends of tape.

3. Fold front seam allowance under so that twill tape does not show, and stitch in place. Leave back seam allowance and twill tape extended.

4. Attach snap fasteners to twill tape.

Bib-front dress

A child's dress with several detachable bibs could eliminate frequent complete changes of clothing. The bib may be lined with terry toweling or plastic. Instructions overleaf.

Detachable bib

Materials:
child's dress
90 cm (1 yd) snap tape for dress and one bib
25 x 27 cm (10 x 11 in) rectangle of matching or contrasting fabric and one of terry toweling or plastic

Instructions:
1. Cut the front neckline opening of the dress to form a square approximately 13 x 13 cm (5½ x 5½ in). Finish the raw edges by applying bias binding or a facing.

2. From the rectangles of dress fabric and terry toweling, cut a bib, following the original neckline and shoulder shape of the dress, and tapering the width from 20 cm (8 in) at the shoulder to 26 cm (10 in) at the lower edge. Place the terry toweling and fabric right sides together and stitch around the edges, leaving an 8 cm (3 in) opening. Trim seams and turn bib. Slipstitch opening. Trim with lace, braid, or rick-rack.

3. A waterproof bib may be constructed by placing a sheet of plastic between the two fabric layers of the bib.

4. Stitch snap tape to the right side of dress and wrong side of bib.

Button-on bib with tie belt

Materials:
child's dress
30 cm (⅓ yd) matching or contrasting fabric
four buttons
optional trim

Instructions:
1. Trace the neckline to the halfway point on the shoulder seam of the dress. From this halfway point, draw a U-shaped bib which extends to the lower chest. Add seam allowances. Cut two bib pieces from this pattern.

2. Placing right sides together, stitch around edges of bib, leaving a 5 cm (2 in) opening to turn the bib through. A trim may be incorporated into this seam if desired.

3. Grade, clip, and notch seam allowances of bib. Turn to right side and press. Slipstitch opening.

4. Make two horizontal buttonholes along the shoulder edge of the bib.

5. Stitch buttons on shoulder of dress to correspond with buttonholes on bib.

6. Construct two ties 2.5 cm (1 in) wide and 75 cm (30 in) long.

7. Attach one tie on each side of bib 6 cm (2½ in) from the bottom. Knot ties in back of dress to hold bib in place.

Blouse with additional yokes

To avoid frequent changes of clothing, additional yokes may be made to fasten on top of the garment yoke. A soiled yoke may then be removed and replaced by a clean one.

Materials:
pattern for blouse with yoke
fabric required for blouse plus 0.45 m (½ yd)

Instructions:
1. Construct blouse as pattern instructions suggest. Use a button closure at center front or back of blouse yoke so that the extra yoke can be attached over the same buttons.

2. Cut two additional yokes using the pattern for the garment yoke.

3. Place the two yokes right sides together. Stitch neck edge at 16 mm (⅝ in) seam allowance, and the outer edges at 13 mm (½ in) so that the yoke is slightly larger than the garment yoke. Leave a 5 cm (2 in) opening at center back.

4. Grade, notch, and understitch yoke seams. Turn yoke right side out and press.

5. Slipstitch opening at center back.

6. Make buttonholes on both ends of yoke to correspond with button closure on blouse.

7. Fasten both ends of detachable yoke over the buttons of the blouse.

Dress with detachable front panel

A child's dress with a detachable front panel is easy to put on and take off because the front is open. The panels can be interchanged without removing the dress.

Materials:
child's collarless dress
0.60 m (⅝ yd) matching or contrasting fabric
0.45 m (½ yd) Velcro
bias tape

Instructions:
1. Mark a line on each side of the dress front, from the intersection of the neckline and shoulder seams to a point on the hemline which is 12 cm (5 in) from the side seam. Slash from neckline to hemline. Bind cut edge with bias tape.

2. Make front panel pattern by following the front neckline curve of the dress to the shoulder, 4 cm (1⅝ in) on the shoulder seam, then tapering from the shoulder to a width of 45 cm (18 in) at the hemline. Add seam allowances and cut two front panels.

3. Stitch Velcro to right side of front panel facing along both seamlines. Stitch front panels, right sides together around sides, shoulder, and neckline, leaving an 8 cm (3 in) opening. Grade seam, clip curve, and trim corners. Turn panel to right side and understitch the panel facing which is the side with the Velcro. Slipstitch lower edge.

4. Stitch Velcro to front edges of dress to correspond to detachable front.

5. Buttons and buttonholes may be used instead of Velcro to fasten front panel.

Dress with detachable sleeve

Frequent changes of clothing due to soiling of the sleeves may be eliminated by the use of detachable sleeves. This garment would be especially useful if combined with a detachable bib or garment front.

Detachable lower sleeves

Materials:
dress with short puffed sleeves and cuff
matching fabric the length of lower sleeve
eight buttons
long-sleeve pattern to fit

Instructions:
1. Measure length of short puffed sleeve from underarm to cuff.

2. Measure same distance on the long sleeve pattern. Draw a line across the long sleeve pattern perpendicular to the grainline. This will become the foldline for the upper edge of the detachable sleeve.

3. To make a facing for the upper edge of the lower sleeve, draw a line 4 cm (1½ in) above the foldline.

4. Cut two lower sleeves.

5. Stitch dart and side seam of detachable sleeve. Hem sleeve.

6. Press top of sleeve under on foldline.

7. Beginning at the side seam, divide the upper edge of the detachable sleeve into quarters. Make a vertical buttonhole at each of the four positions.

8. Attach four buttons to the right side of the cuff of the dress to correspond with the buttonholes of the detachable sleeve.

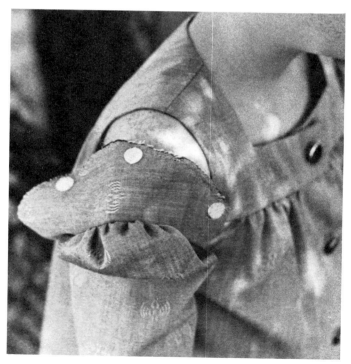

Detachable sleeves

Child's wheelchair bib

Materials:
pattern for long-sleeved dress
fabric and notions required
Velcro discs

A bib which fits around a child and the wheelchair serves as both a bib and a sturdy belt to hold the child comfortably and securely in the chair. Straps fastened with metal loops and Velcro may be adjusted to fit a child of any size. Instructions overleaf.

Instructions:
1. Following the curve of the bodice armhole, trace a facing pattern 5 cm (2 in) wide at shoulder and 2 cm (¾ in) wide at underarm.

2. Cut two facings.

3. Stitch underarm seam of facing.

4. Construct sleeve as pattern instructions direct.

5. Set sleeve into facing and finish raw edge of facing.

6. Divide the facing into quarters and attach a Velcro disc at each quarter point.

7. Construct the garment as pattern instructions direct, omitting sleeves.

8. Cut a bias strip of fabric 2 cm (¾ in) wide and the circumference of the armhole long.

9. Bind the garment armhole with the bias strip.

10. Attach several Velcro discs to the inside of the garment armhole so that they match the discs on the facing. When attached, the sleeve should look like an ordinary set-in sleeve.

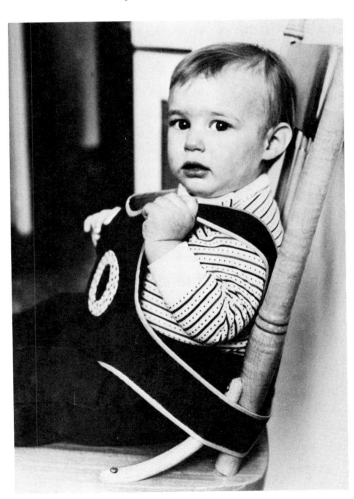

Materials:

0.45 m (½ yd) sturdy fabric
5 m (5½ yd) double-fold bias tape
four metal loops
5 cm Velcro

Instructions:

1. Enlarge pattern to scale. The length of the bib from A to B should be the body measurement from neckline to crotch. Piece the strap extensions of the pattern to fit onto the fabric.

2. Stitch strap extensions to straps.

3. Finish all edges of bib and straps with double-fold bias tape.

4. Stitch Velcro to waist straps to fit around the child and the wheelchair.

5. Thread each lower strap through two metal loops. Fold strap over loops and stitch in place.

6. To secure child in chair, fasten waist straps, then thread shoulder straps through loops on lower straps and pull tight.

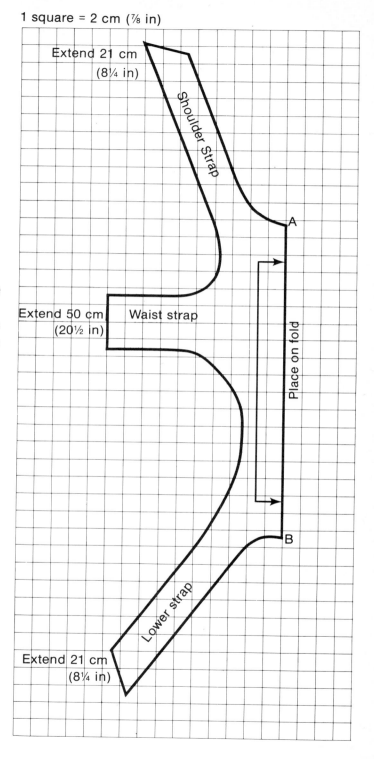

1 square = 2 cm (⅞ in)

Extend 21 cm (8¼ in)

Shoulder Strap

A

Extend 50 cm (20½ in)

Waist strap

Place on fold

B

Lower strap

Extend 21 cm (8¼ in)

Reversible back-wrapped jumper with matching pants for child with congenital hip problem

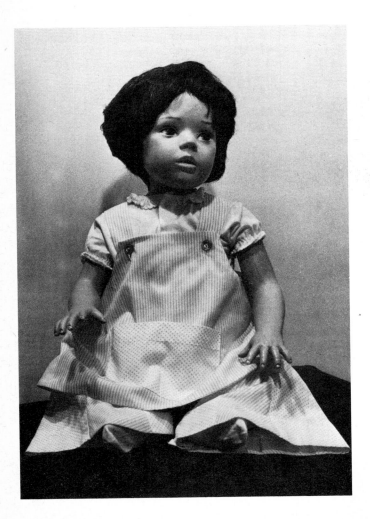

Children with congenital hip problems may be required to wear special braces which keep the child in a "frog" position. Dressing and undressing children wearing such a brace is difficult. Conventional garments do not provide the room nor the wearability to accommodate the prosthesis.

Commercial patterns such as the one illustrated may be adapted to provide more comfort for the child and greater ease in dressing.

Garment features

Reversible jumper
- longer wearing.
- wrap-around, lapping over at the back to provide additional room for braces and freedom of movement.
- easy-to-fasten button straps on jumper.
- pockets and shaped front bib.

Pants

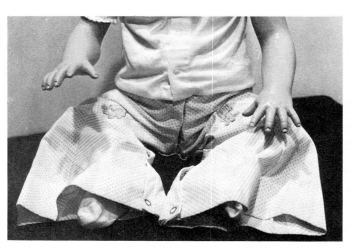

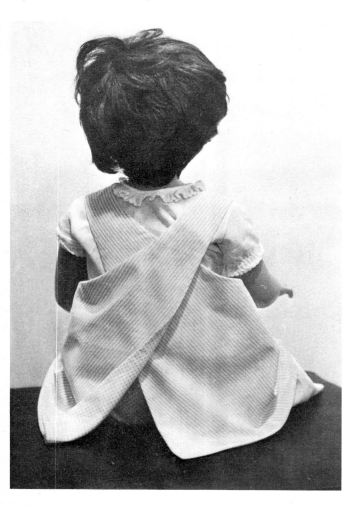

- triangular bias inserts set in pant legs provide additional room for braces and ease of movement.
- legs of pants are terry cloth lined to increase absorbency and decrease wear due to abrasion from braces.
- elasticized waist facilitates dressing and adjusts to size of child.
- snaps along inner pant legs, and front crotch to waist, allow pants to open out flat for ease of dressing.

8. Bathing suits

Two-piece bathing suits

A garment that has a front opening or opens
out flat eliminates the need to struggle
with a back opening or with a step-in garment.

To many handicapped individuals swimming
is a form of therapy. It is therefore important
to find various styles of bathing suits
which can be made or altered to suit specific
needs. Some women find a two-piece bathing
suit more comfortable to wear and easier
to put on. Others prefer the one-piece.
Likewise, some prefer front closures while for
the person requiring assistance in dressing,
the back closure may be more desirable.

Materials:
commercial pattern for two-piece bathing suit
fabric as required
three 15 mm (½ in) buttons
four 4 cm (1½ in) plastic rings

Instructions:
Bra
1. Cut back piece on fold, eliminating back opening.

2. Extend center front line 5 cm (2 in) so that the bra may be buttoned in front.

3. On front pieces, fold 4 cm (1½ in) under for facing. Otherwise construct bra as pattern directs.

4. Construct three buttonholes and sew buttons to front opening.

Bottoms
1. Add a 8 cm (3 in) extension to side seam of back panel.

2. Add a 5 cm (2 in) extension to side seam of front panel.

3. Construct bottoms, but do not join front and back at side seams.

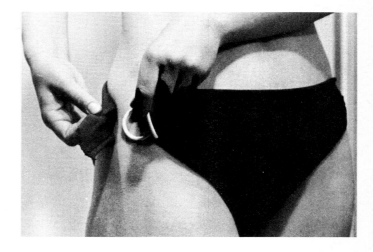

4. Insert two rings in each front extension and fasten extension to form a loop.

5. The back extension is then threaded through the rings to secure the bottoms in place.

A halter top which laps at the back and ties in front may be fastened by a person who has only the use of one arm or one who cannot manipulate small closures.

The bottoms open out flat and are closed with snaps or Velcro.

Bathing suit for a post-mastectomy patient

Bathing suit with front zipper

A bathing suit which is cut high in the front and arm area is most suitable for a woman who has had a mastectomy. The bra cup may be padded with fiberfill to give a natural outline.

A front zipper may be added to a one-piece bathing suit for ease in dressing. Instructions overleaf.

Materials:
bathing suit with bra cup

or

pattern and fabric as required
fiberfill
0.20 m (¼ yd) lingerie tricot

Instructions:
1. Fill the bra cup with fiberfill to fit the body.

2. Stitch a piece of lingerie tricot over the bra cup to hold the fiberfill in place.

Materials:
one-piece bathing suit
45 cm (18 in) zipper
50 x 10 cm (20 x 4 in) strip of fabric

Instructions:
1. Center zipper on center front line, folding upper edge under even with neckline edge, and topstitch into place along tape edges.

2. Slash underneath zipper teeth to within 13 mm (½ in) of end of zipper, then slash diagonally to ends of stitching to form a triangle.

3. Turn lower ends of zipper and triangle at bottom of slash to the inside. Stitch through zipper tape and triangle across the lower end of zipper from the wrong side.

4. An inset is needed to protect the body from the abrasive action of the zipper. Fold the strip of fabric lengthwise, right sides together, and stitch across the upper end. Trim and turn.

5. Baste inset underneath zipper matching edge to zipper tape and neckline curve. Topstitch through zipper and inset along edge of zipper tape and lower end of the first stitching line.

6. Stitch lower edge of inset to crotch seam to hold inset smoothly in place.

Note: A bathing suit with a zipper in the center back crotch seam may prove valuable for a dependent handicapped who requires assistance in dressing.

162

Girl's bathing suit

For ease of dressing, a girl's bathing suit may be altered to open out flat.

Materials:
two-piece bathing suit
1 m (1 yd) of 2 cm (¾ in) twill tape
13 snap fasteners

Instructions:
1. Remove stitching in both side seams of shorts and one seam of top.

2. On front piece of shorts bind edges with twill tape, turning ends inside. Fold tape to the inside and stitch in place.

3. On back piece, bind edges with twill tape, folding under ends, and leaving tape extended.

4. Attach five snap fasteners to close each side seam.

5. Follow same procedure for one side seam of bathing suit top.

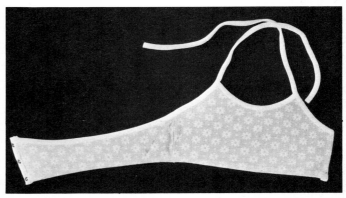

Bathing trunks

Bathing trunks may be adapted to open out flat by inserting separating zippers in the side seams. This makes it easier for someone else to dress the person.

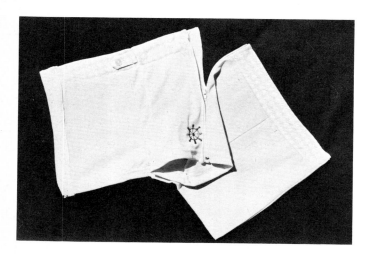

Materials:
bathing trunks
two 25 cm (10 in) separating zippers
two 28 cm (11 in) strips of polyester knit tubing, approximately 1.3 cm (½ in) wide
two 28 x 6 cm (11 x 2½ in) strips of knit fabric

Instructions:
1. Remove stitching in side seams. Press under 6 mm (¼ in) seam allowance.

2. Stitch separating zipper into side seam, leaving zipper teeth exposed.

3. Turn in ends of knit tubing. Topstitch to front of trunks so that it laps toward the back and covers the zipper.

4. Fold strip of knit fabric in half lengthwise and stitch ends. Trim and turn to right side. Stitch inset to front zipper tape so that it laps backward to protect the body from the abrasive action of the zipper.

Trunks with envelope for catheter bag

This pair of men's bathing trunks has a separating zipper on either side so that the garment opens out flat. In addition across the front abdomen area is a fold of fabric into which a catheter bag can be inserted.

Materials:
pair of bathing trunks
2 separating zippers same color as the trunks and as long as the side seams
lightweight fabric approximately 30 cm (12 in) long by 23 cm (9 in) wide. This should be slightly larger than twice the size of the catheter bag used.

Instructions:
1. Open side seams and the front waistline hem.

2. Hem short sides of lightweight fabric. Press. Fold in two so that long sides are together. Slip raw edges under the waistline band at the top of the front section on the inside of the trunks and stitch. The fold of fabric will hang free from the front waistband.

3. Insert separating zippers on each side with separating end at the lower edge of trunks.

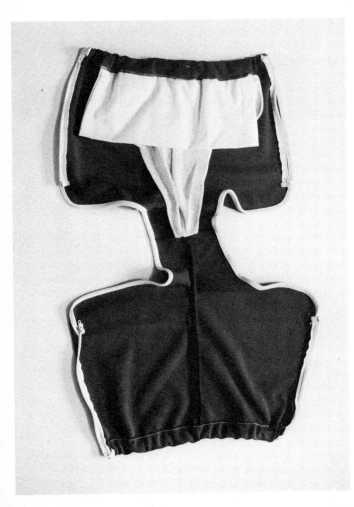

Terry cloth robe

A terry cloth beach robe can double as an attractive cover-up for a person taking therapy. Its wrap-around design and loose cape sleeves combine for ease in dressing.

Materials:
2 m (2⅛ yd) of 115 cm (45 in) fabric
8.30 m (9 yd) bias binding
0.30 m (⅓ yd) cotton for pocket lining

Instructions:
1. Stitch top of pocket lining to top of pocket, right sides together, leaving a 5 cm (2 in) opening. Fold pocket and pocket lining, right sides together, so that curved edges match, and stitch around edges. Grade and notch seam allowances. Turn pocket right side out through opening. Press. Slipstitch opening.

2. Pin pockets to fronts in position comfortable to wearer. Topstitch close to the edge, reinforcing upper corners by stitching small triangles.

3. Join back to fronts at shoulder and side seams. Press seams open.

4. Bind raw edges of robe with double-fold bias tape.

5. Finish raw edges of armhole and sleeve in the above manner.

6. Place sleeve under armhole edge so that bound edges meet, matching the center of the sleeve to the shoulder seam. Topstitch close to binding to attach sleeve.

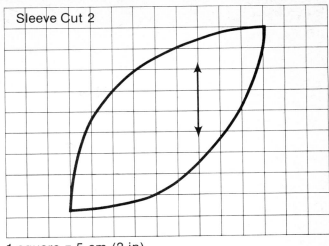

Sleeve Cut 2

1 square = 5 cm (2 in)

7. Cut four belt sections. Join sections to form two long strips. Trim seam and press open. Match the two pieces, right sides together, and stitch around edges, leaving a 10 cm (4 in) opening. Grade seam, trim corners, and turn to right side. Slipstitch opening. Belt loops may be applied to the side seams or the belt may be worn threaded through the back and tied in front.

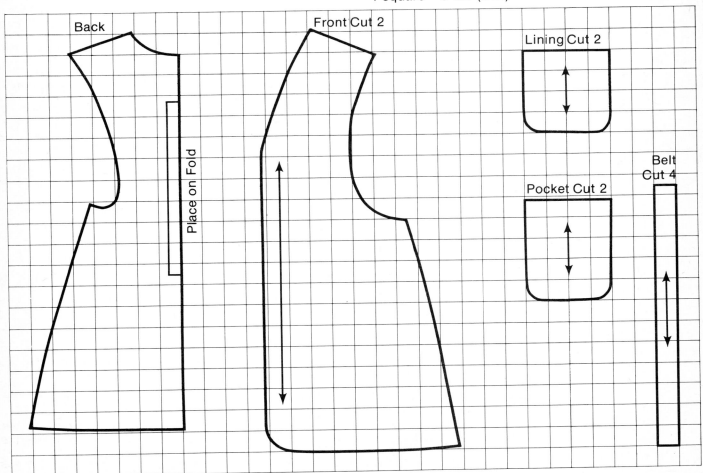

Back

Front Cut 2

Place on Fold

Lining Cut 2

Pocket Cut 2

Belt Cut 4

9. Wheelchair wraps

Separating wheelchair wrap

Materials:
3.70 m (4 yd) 115 cm (45 in) fabric
3.70 m (4 yd) 115 cm (45 in) quilted lining
18.30 m (20 yd) 2.5 cm (1 in) braid
7.50 cm (3 in) Velcro
metallic clasp
two 50 cm (20 in) zippers
one 30 cm (12 in) separating zipper
one 90 cm (36 in) separating zipper
one 2 m (80 in) separating zipper

This wheelchair wrap has a horizontal waist-high separating zipper which enables the cape to be worn by itself. It has a quilted lining for warmth.

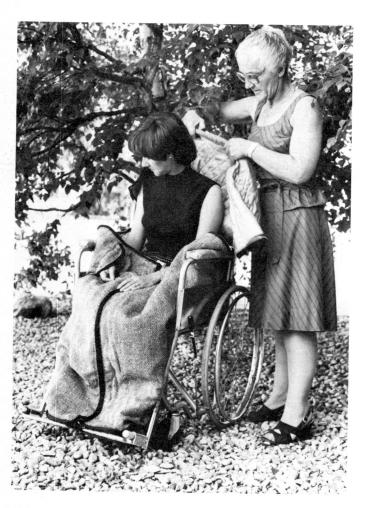

Instructions:
To lengthen or shorten body section of wrap, slash on lines CD and spread or overlap needed amount. Redraw cutting lines and line AB. The wrap should be 26 to 30 cm (10 to 12 in) longer than the person wearing the wrap.

Cape
1. Join front to back at side seams of fabric. Repeat for quilted lining.

2. Baste the two collar sections, wrong sides together, being sure to roll the collar so that the undercollar is smaller than the upper collar. Enclose raw outside edges in braid.

3. Stitch collars to the cape neckline. Press seam allowances downward.

4. Baste lining to wrong side of cape, matching seams.

5. Turn neckline edge of lining under along neckline edge of cape and handstitch in place.

6. Apply braid to enclose raw edges.
(*Continued on page 172*)

1 square = 5 cm (2 in)

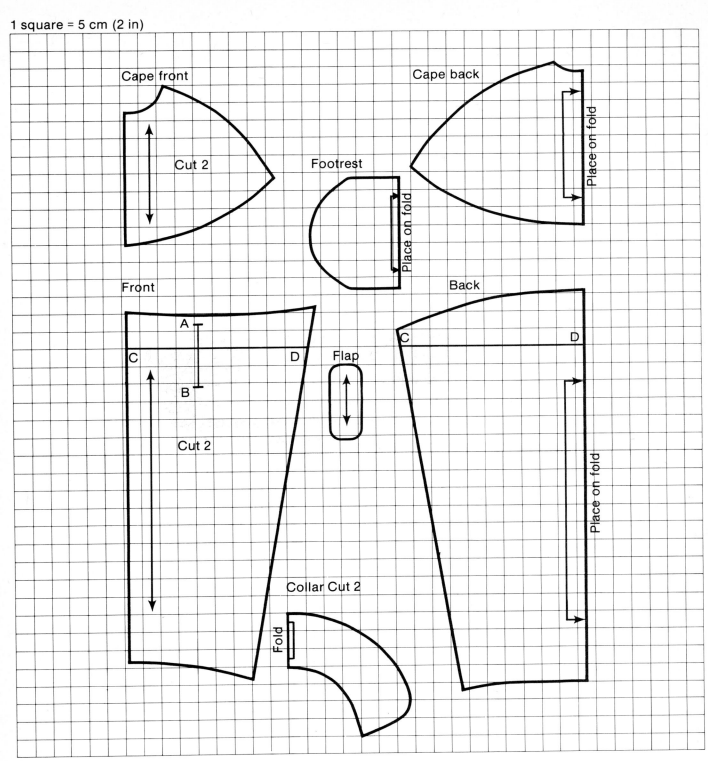

Cape front

Cut 2

Footrest

Place on fold

Cape back

Place on fold

Front

A

B

C

D

Cut 2

Flap

Back

C

D

Place on fold

Collar Cut 2

Fold

7. Insert 30 cm (12 in) separating zipper in front opening, beginning about 9 cm (3½ in) below the neckline.

8. Thread a 4 cm (1½ in) strip of braid through the end of each half of the magnetic clasp and sew in place at the neckline.

Body

1. Construct a bound buttonhole on the line AB in each front to serve as a slot opening for the arms.

2. Fold flap in half, wrong sides together, and enclose raw edges with braid. Handstitch flap to the edge of slot opening farthest from center front, so that the flap covers the opening.

3. Join fronts to back at side seams of fabric, and of lining.

4. Place wrong sides of body and body lining together, matching seams, and baste. Slash the slot opening in the lining, fold over and handstitch it to the edges of the bound buttonhole.

5. Enclose all raw edges with braid.

6. Insert 90 cm (36 in) separating zipper in front opening, beginning approximately 8 cm (3 in) from top of body section.

7. Attach Velcro above zipper.

8. Insert 2 m (80 in) separating zipper to join cape to body of the wrap.

Foot rest

1. Baste fabric and lining wrong sides together.

2. Enclose raw edges with braid.

3. Join foot rest to body at center back using a 30 cm (12 in) strip of braid sewn to each braid edge.

4. Insert a 50 cm (20 in) zipper from each side to back closing to center front to attach the foot rest to the body of the wrap.

172

Wheelchair wrap with front panel

A wheelchair wrap designed like a bunting bag keeps a person warm and minimizes constriction. The two zippers allow the wrap to be opened out on the chair before the wearer is seated. The front panel may be opened for ventilation without removing the entire garment. A detachable pile lining can be used in cold weather. If desired, anchor ties may be sewn on the outside at seat level to anchor and position the wrap on the chair. Inside ties hold the person in proper position. Instructions overleaf.

Materials:

3.70 m (4 yd) of 115 cm (45 in) fabric
3.70 m (4 yd) of 115 cm (45 in) pile lining
two 140 cm (55 in) heavyweight zippers
24 snaps
2.80 m (3 yd) bias tape
2.20 m (2⅜ yd) of 2.5 cm (1 in) twill tape
0.45 m (½ yd) of 3 mm (⅛ in) elastic

Instructions:

A suitable length for the wrap is 26 to 36 cm (10 to 14 in) longer than the height of the person to wear the wrap. If more or less length is required, slash along line ST, and spread or overlap needed amount. Redraw cutting lines, maintaining smooth curves and straight lines.

1. With right sides together, sew line AB in a dart shape at center back.

2. For arm opening slash on line NO on the front panel, and bind the raw edges with bias strips. At both top N and lower O edges of arm opening, reinforce by stitching.

3. Slash on line PQ to form zipper openings. Turn under raw edge 6 mm (¼ in). Center zipper in opening and topstitch close to folded edge.

4. Join back and front pieces at side seams by sewing line CD to line IJ.

5. Connect the back and front pieces at the bottom of the wrap by stitching line FG to line LM.

6. Join the sides of the bottom by sewing line EDJK to line EFLK.

7. Finish neck edge of wrap and of center panel as desired.

Anchor ties and waistline ties

8. In order to position the wrap correctly and to prevent it from slipping, apply anchor ties on the outside to hold the wrap to the chair and a waistline tie on the inside to keep the body in place. Have the person sit in the wrap in the chair to determine the correct position for the ties and their required length.

9. Cut a strip of fabric 10 x 127 cm (4 x 50 in) for anchor ties. Cut two pieces of 2.5 cm (1 in) twill tape, 56 cm (22 in) long.

10. To make the inside ties, turn the ends of the twill tape under 1 cm (⅜ in) and stitch. Baste ties on inside at position determined above and about 12 cm (5 in) on either side of center back. This tie will only be used when the lining is removed. (*Continued on page 176*)

1 square = 5 cm (2 in)

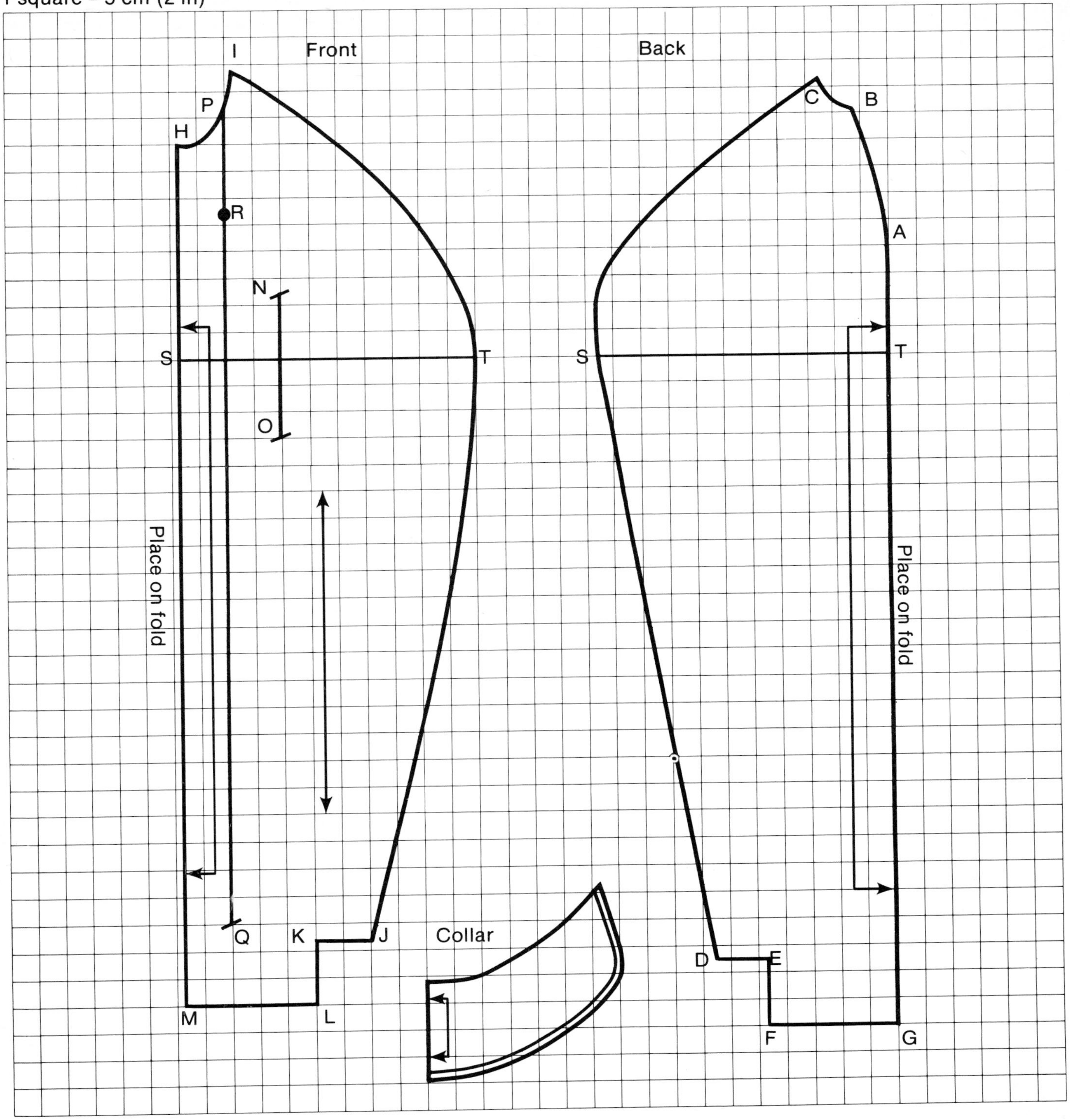

I Front Back

P
H C B
R A
N
S T S T
O

Place on fold Place on fold

Q K J Collar
M L D E
F G

175

11. To construct the anchor tie, fold the strip of fabric in half lengthwise, right sides together, and stitch the side and one end. Turn right side out and finish open end. Position on the right side at the same points as the inside ties were placed. Fasten the anchor tie and the inside ties securely by topstitching through all layers. Stitch Velcro on the ends of the anchor tie so that it fastens behind the chair.

Lining

12. Construct the pile lining, following steps 1 to 7 above except for zippers. Bind raw edges of lining at zipper openings, neckline, and armhole opening.

13. An inside tie on the lining may be necessary to hold the body in place. Follow Step 8 above.

Collar

14. Cut one collar from the pile fabric. Turn under outer edge of collar and stitch. Bind inner edge of collar with bias tape. Stitch elastic to bias tape to ease inner edge of collar. Handstitch collar to neckline, matching ends of collar to point R.

15. Apply snaps along zipper, neckline, and armhole openings to fasten lining to outer shell.

Hooded wheelchair wrap

Urethane-coated nylon makes a lightweight and waterproof wheelchair wrap. The waistline ties on the inside hold the person who might slip down in the chair. The anchor ties on the outside tie around the back of the chair to correctly position the wrap. The entire wrap folds into a pocket which forms a carrying pouch that hooks on the back of the wheelchair. A pile lining can be snapped in place to add extra warmth. Instructions overleaf.

Materials:

4 m (4¼ yd) 115 cm (45 in) fabric
155 cm (62 in) zipper, heavy weight
150 cm (60 in) cord for drawstring
8 cm (3 in) Velcro

Instructions:

1. To increase or decrease length, slash and spread or overlap needed amount on line ST. Redraw cutting edges to form smooth curves. The wrap should be 15 to 30 cm (6 to 12 in) longer than the height of the wearer.

2. Put right sides together and sew line AB in the dart shape.

3. The slot opening for arms, line NO, should be positioned to suit the wearer and constructed as either a machine or bound buttonhole.

4. Insert zipper in center front opening, line HM.

5. Join back and front pieces at side seams by sewing line CD to line IJ.

6. Connect the back and front pieces at the bottom of the wrap by stitching line FG to line LM.

7. Join the sides of the bottom by sewing line EDJK and line EFLK. This produces a flat, squared area for the feet.

8. Sew darts in hood section.

9. Join hood sections by stitching line PQ.

10. Construct a machine buttonhole on either side of the hood in order to insert a drawstring. The buttonhole should be parallel to the neckline and approximately 3 cm (1⅛ in) from the front edge and 2 cm (¾ in) from the lower edge.

11. Turn under a 2.5 cm (1 in) hem around the front edge of the hood and stitch to form a casing. Insert the drawstring through the buttonholes and thread it through the casing.

12. Join hood neckline QR to the garment neckline HICB. The seam allowances may be machine overcast together so that no facing is necessary.

13. In order to position the wrap correctly and to prevent it from slipping, apply anchor ties on the outside to hold the wrap to the chair, and waistline ties on the inside to keep the body in place. See instructions for wheelchair wrap with front panel 8 to 11 inclusive.

14. A removable lining may be made from the same pattern and snapped into the wrap for added warmth. See instructions for wheelchair wrap with front panel, page 173.

1 square = 5 cm (2 in)

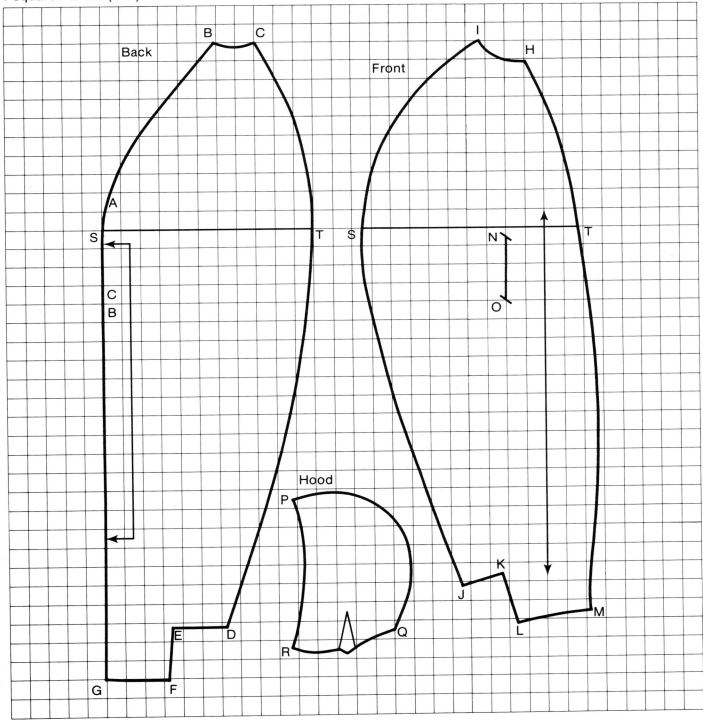

Back

B   C

Front

I   H

A

S   T S   N   T

C
B   O

Hood

P

K
J
E D   Q   L   M
R
G F

10. Pattern alterations for person in sitting position

The posture of a seated person is much different from the standing posture. The back length is increased because it is curved, while the front length is decreased. A person who is confined to a wheelchair would be more comfortable and attractive if his clothes were fitted to accommodate the seated posture. The figures used in the following pattern alterations are guidelines for the average person, and may have to be altered through experimentation to suit the individual.

Suit jacket

A person who is seated has a shorter front length. This causes a standard bodice front to form folds of excess fabric across the chest and above the waistline. The neckline gapes because of the forward posture.

Instructions for altering a jacket to take account of a constant sitting position follow overleaf.

Bodice front

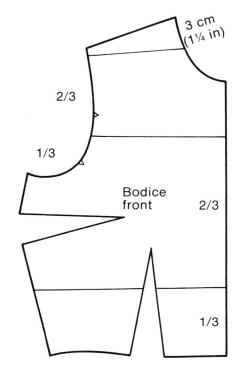

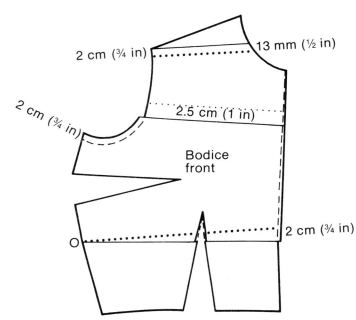

1. To decrease the front bodice length, mark three slash lines perpendicular to the lengthwise grainline. The first line is 3 cm (1¼ in) below the shoulder seam at the neckline. The second is positioned 2/3 down the armhole curve and the third is 2/3 of the distance down the bodice from the second slash.

2. Overlap upper slash 2 cm (¾ in) at the armhole, tapering to 13 mm (½ in) at neckline. The second line is overlapped evenly, 25 mm (1 in) from armhole to center front. The third overlap tapers from 2 cm (¾ in) at center front to zero at the side seam.

3. The new center front seam is a smooth, slightly curved line.

4. Drop the armhole curve 2 cm (¾ in) to compensate for the shortening done above.

Bodice back

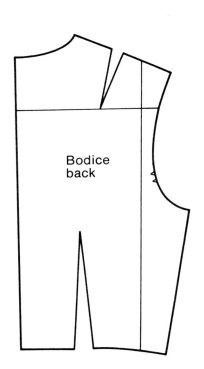

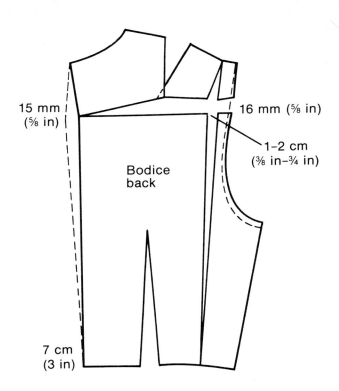

When a person is seated the back and shoulder are curved, causing the bodice back to pull up and strain across the shoulders.

1. Draw a line perpendicular to the lengthwise grainline at the bottom of the shoulder dart, from center back to the armhole. From the armhole slash to, but not through, center back seam. Slash through the center of the dart from the shoulder to the point of the dart. Spread slash 15 mm (⅝ in) at the armhole. The new shoulder dart will be wider than the original.

2. A person using a wheelchair develops his upper back muscle causing even more strain across the shoulders in the bodice back. To alleviate this, draw a line parallel to the lengthwise grainline from shoulder to waistline. Slash to but not through the shoulder and waistline. Spread the slash 1–2 cm (⅜–¾ in) at the slash below the shoulder dart. True the shoulder seam.

3. The center back seam is curved outwards to add width. Mark 15 mm (⅝ in) outside of center back at the perpendicular slash line. Draw a line from 7 cm (2¾ in) above the waistline to this point, then curve the line toward the neckline.

4. Drop the underarm curve to match the altered bodice front, then true the armhole curve.

Collar

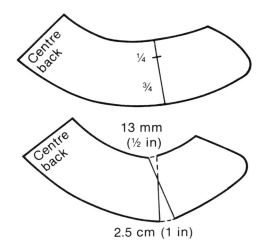

13 mm
(½ in)

Centre back

2.5 cm (1 in)

The collar tends to stand away from the neck because of the forward posture. The collar needs to be shortened at the neckline the same amount as the neckline of the front bodice was shortened.

1. At the shoulder, draw a line from the neckline to the edge of the collar pattern. Mark a point on this line which is ¼ of the distance from the neckline.

2. Slash from the neckline to but not through this point, and from the edge of the collar to but not through this point. Pivot the collar pieces so that the collar neckline is decreased by 13 mm (½ in).

Sleeve

The arm of the person in a wheelchair is normally bent, causing excess folds of fabric at the elbow. The following alteration is only possible with a two-piece sleeve.

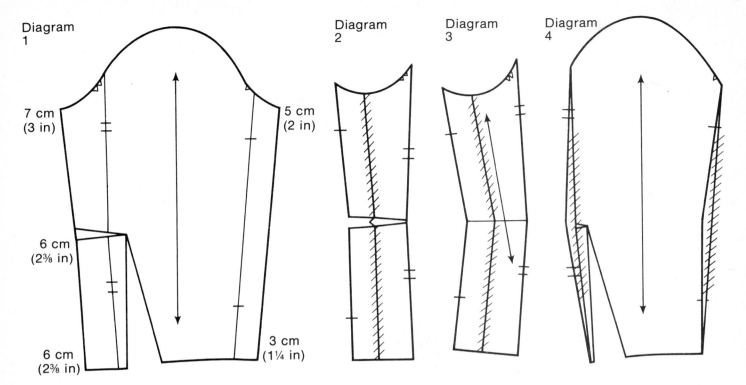

Diagram 1

Diagram 2

Diagram 3

Diagram 4

7 cm (3 in)

5 cm (2 in)

6 cm (2⅜ in)

6 cm (2⅜ in)

3 cm (1¼ in)

To make a two-piece sleeve

1. Slash through elbow dart and to the wrist. Fold out half of the dart to increase width at the wrist. Place a piece of paper under the spread and tape in place.

2. Fold out remainder of dart and draw new seam lines (see Diagram 1). Put matching notches on these seamlines.

3. Open dart. Cut sleeve apart at seamlines.

4. Join front and back underarm sections at the original seamline. To make front and back pieces match, cut front so that it will spread open at the dart (see Diagram 2).

5. Redraw the elbow dart, extending through back and front underarm sleeve. Fold out dart, giving a forward slant to the lower end of the sleeve (see Diagram 3).

6. Redraw the front seam of the upper sleeve as a curve that takes off about 2 cm (¾ in) at the elbow. Redraw the back seam adding about 2 cm (¾ in) at the elbow thus regaining the original width at the elbow (see Diagram 4).

7. Add 16 mm (⅝ in) seam allowances to the new seamlines.

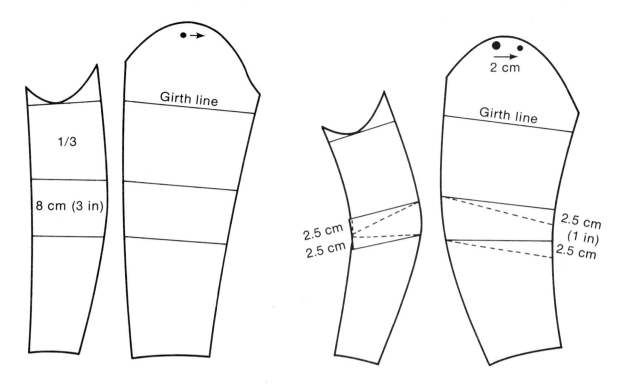

To alter a two-piece sleeve

1. Draw a line perpendicular to the lengthwise grainline, 4 cm (1½ in) on each side of the elbow on both pattern pieces.

2. Slash from the front seam of each pattern piece to, but not through the back seam, on both lines. Overlap 25 mm (1 in) on each line so that the pattern piece curves forward.

3. Move the top of shoulder dot 2 cm (¾ in) to the front. This will cause the sleeve to swing forward.

Skirt

Excess folds of fabric form on the skirt front
in the lap area when a person is seated. The
skirt needs to be shortened at center front.
Instructions overleaf.

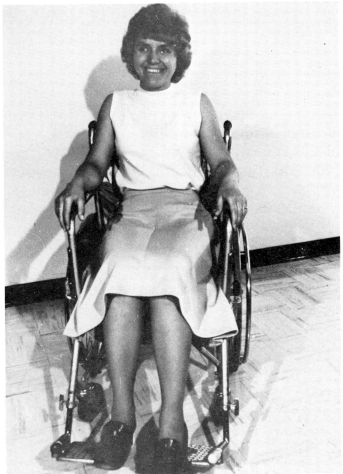

Skirt front

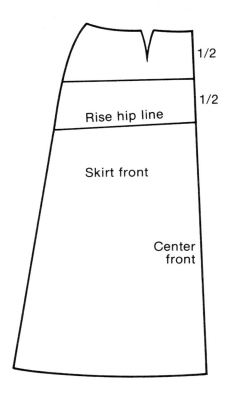

1. Draw a perpendicular line to center front at the fullest part of the hip (called the hip rise line). Draw a second line which divides the pattern above the hip rise line in half. Slash from center front on each line to, but not through, the side seam. Overlap the pattern pieces so that the two slash lines meet at center front.

2. Redraw the distorted center front seam to form a smooth curve.

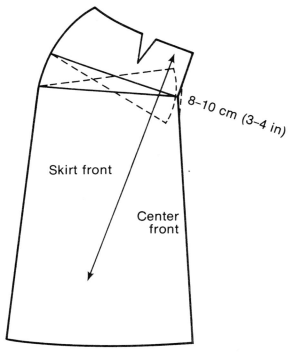

Skirt back

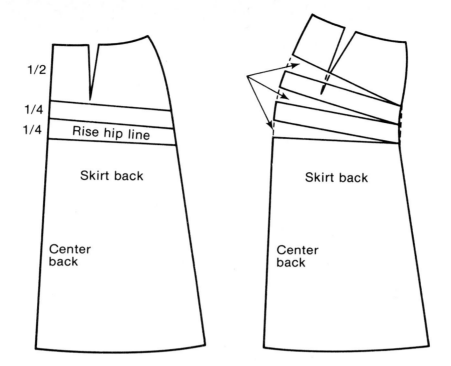

The skirt rides up in the back to cover the additional back length created by sitting. Length should be added at center back.

1. Mark the hip rise line at the fullest part of the hip, perpendicular to center back. Draw a second line which divides the skirt above the hip rise line in half. Draw a third line which divides the space between the first two lines in half.

2. Slash from center back to, but not through the side seam, on the three lines. Spread each slash 2–4 cm (¾–1½ in), depending on the body shape.

3. Redraw the center back and side seams to form a smooth curve.

Slacks

A fold of fabric forms in the front of slacks when a person is seated. The center front should be shortened to eliminate the extra fabric.

Slacks front

Diagram 1

C

A   D   B

Rise hip line

7–10 cm
(3–4 in)

Pants front

Diagram 2

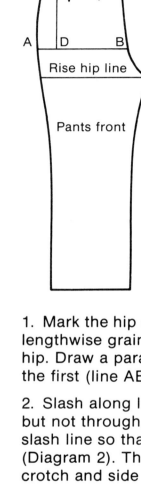

Pants front

1. Mark the hip rise line perpendicular to the lengthwise grainline at the fullest part of the hip. Draw a parallel line 7–10 cm above the first (line AB).

2. Slash along line AB from center front, to but not through, the side seam. Overlap the slash line so that it meets the hip rise line (Diagram 2). This alteration causes both crotch and side seams to be more curved.

3. Smooth out the front crotch and side seams at point of alteration.

4. If abdomen is flat, shift front waistline darts toward the side seams to create a more pleasing appearance.

Slacks back

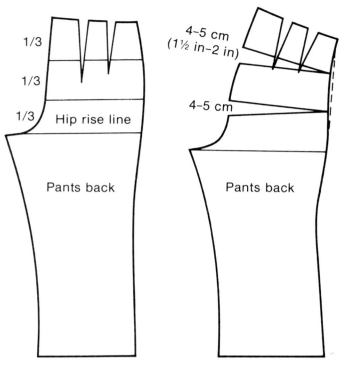

1/3

1/3

1/3 Hip rise line

Pants back

4–5 cm
(1½ in–2 in)

4–5 cm

Pants back

When a person is seated, slacks are too short in the back, causing the back waistline to pull down and gape. Extra length should be added to allow the waistband to sit in the proper position.

1. Mark the hip rise line perpendicular to the lengthwise grainline, at the fullest part of the hips. Draw two parallel lines dividing the pattern above the rise line into thirds.

2. Slash from center front to but not through the side seam on the upper two lines. Spread the two slashes 4–5 cm (1½–2 in), depending on the body shape.

3. Redraw the center back and side seams to form smooth curves.

194

Cape

A cape is a very practical outer garment for a person in a wheelchair because it gives warmth without being constricting. This cape and skirt have been modified to look their best in a seated position. The cape is shortened at the back so that the person doesn't sit on it. The skirt is lengthened at the back to conform to the contours of the body in a seated position.

 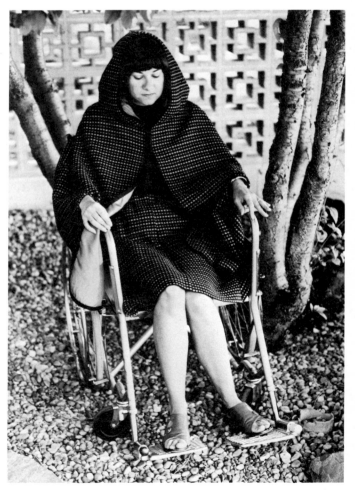

11. Miscellaneous

Car slide

A slide is an aid to persons who have difficulty getting positioned properly on a car seat. The person sits on the slide and someone else can then easily pull him along the seat.

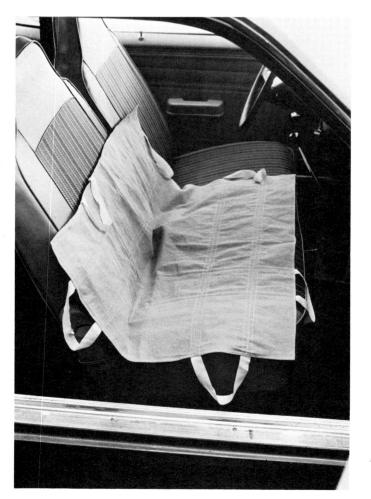

Materials:
0.80 m (⅞ yd) nylon
0.80 m (⅞ yd) denim (pre-washed)
0.45 m (½ yd) of 150 cm (60 in) firm, strong fabric

The side of the slide which is placed against the car seat should be a smooth, slippery fabric such as nylon. The side that the person sits on should be a firm, non-slippery fabric such as denim to prevent the person from slipping.

Instructions:
1. Cut the 0.45 m piece of fabric into 7 cm (2¾ in) wide strips. Join these strips into one long strip. Fold in half lengthwise, with right sides together, and stitch long side, using a 1 cm (⅜ in) seam allowance. Grade seam and turn to right side. Press.

2. Lay the strip of fabric on the wrong side of the non-slippery piece of fabric as shown in Diagram. Fasten it in place by a row of stitching.

3. Put the slippery piece of fabric against the non-slippery fabric, wrong sides together. Secure the edges by zig-zagging or sewing a number of rows of straight stitching very close together.

4. Secure the strips of fabric by stitching down the center of the strip through both layers of fabric. Either a zig-zag stitch or a number of rows of straight stitching very close together can be used.

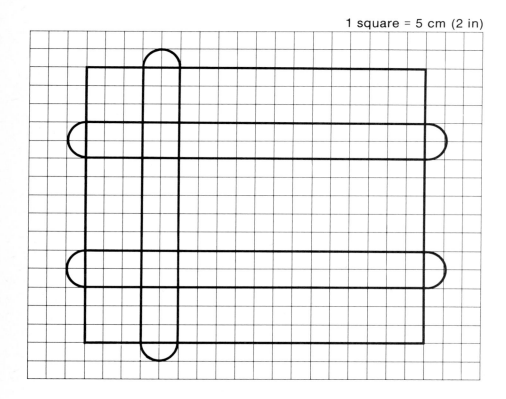

1 square = 5 cm (2 in)

Lap tray

It is difficult for a person in a wheelchair to balance objects on the lap. A cloth tray with stiffened edges can be constructed to provide a flat surface on which to place articles. The stiffened edge serves to prevent things from slipping off the tray.

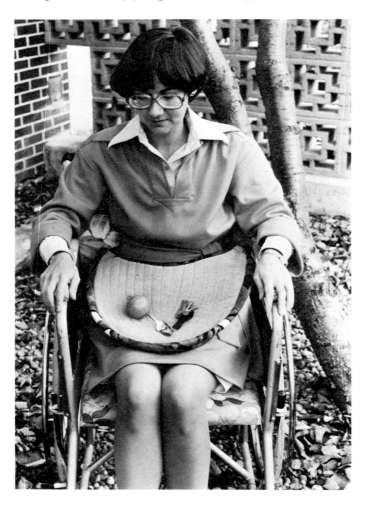

Materials:
1 m (1⅛ yd) fabric

or

0.45 m (½ yd) each of two contrasting fabrics, and 0.45 m (½ yd) padding fabric
3 cm (1 in) Velcro
1 m (1⅛ yd) rubber tubing (e.g. garden hose)

Instructions:
1. Using the accompanying pattern, cut two pieces from the outer fabric and one from the padding fabric. If contrasting fabric is used, cut one piece from each fabric.

2. Position the three layers, one on top of the other, with the padding fabric in the middle. Baste together near the outside edges.

3. Quilt the tray surface by stitching through all layers 16 mm (⅝ in) from the cut edge. Stitch consecutive rows 16 mm (⅝ in) inside the first row until the entire surface is quilted.

4. Cut bias strips of fabric 8 cm (3 in) wide and join as needed to form a strip 115 cm (44 in) long.

5. Bind outer edge of tray, turning all raw edges under but leaving ends open.

6. Cut bias strips 4 cm (1½ in) wide and join to form a strip 45 cm (18 in) long.

7. Bind inner edge of tray, turning raw edges under.

1 square = 5 cm (2 in)

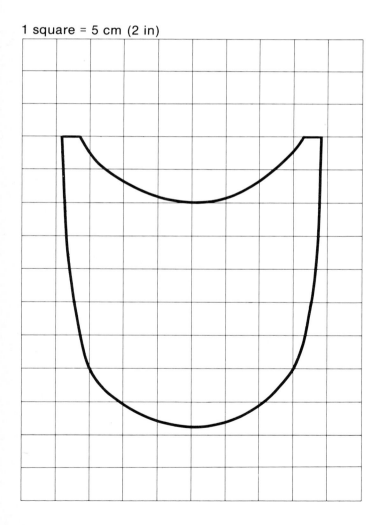

8. Cut a strip of fabric 8 cm (3 in) wide to form a back band for the tray. The band should be of sufficient length to fasten around the back waist and hold the tray in place.

9. Attach the band to one end of the tray, leaving the outer binding free.

10. Attach Velcro to the other end of the tray and the free end of the band.

11. Cut the ends of the rubber tubing at an angle.

12. Insert the tubing into the outer binding with the longer side to the inside. Close the ends of binding with hand stitching.

Note: If the rubber tubing is found to be too heavy, it can be replaced with copper wire. Reinforcement may be omitted if the outer edge bias strip is highly stretched as it is applied to the tray fabric.

Lap throw

A lap throw can be put on while the person is sitting in a chair to keep the lower part of the body warm. The pockets serve as hand-warmers as well as providing a place to put things.

Materials:
1 m (1⅛ yd) soft, lightweight knit fabric

or

blanket, cut to the proper size
decorative trim (fringe, braid, etc.)

Instructions:
1. Cut the fabric using the pattern given. If a rather lightweight fabric is used and you wish to use a double thickness of it, cut two pieces of fabric from the pattern. Cut the pocket pieces.

2. Finish the raw edges of the throw with the decorative trim.

3. Finish the raw edges of the pockets and stitch them onto the throw. Depending on what the pockets are to be used for, they can be positioned to open towards center front, side, or top of throw.

1 square = 10 cm (4 in)

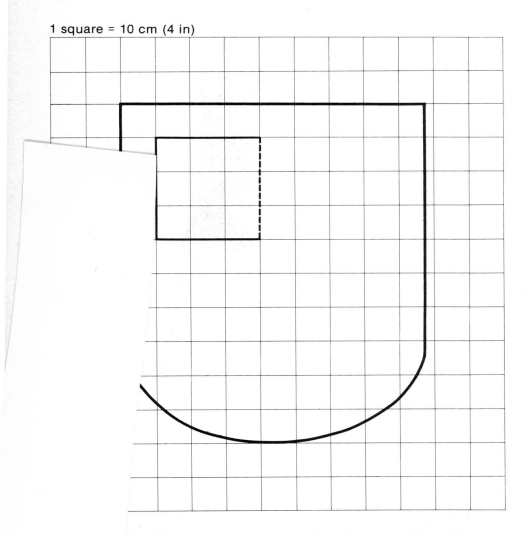

Shawl

Extra warmth may be gained with a minimum of difficulty in dressing by placing a shawl around the shoulders. Large pockets are located in a convenient position.

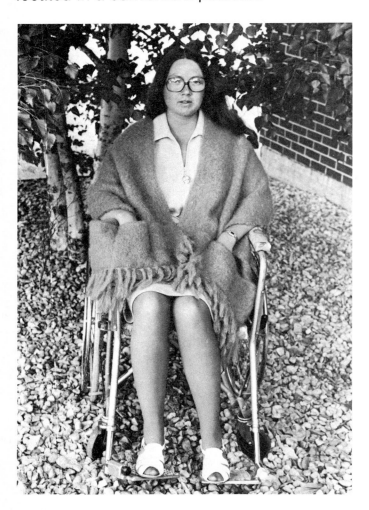

Materials:
two mohair scarves approximately 160 x 50 cm (62 x 20 in)

or

two rectangles of fabric 160 x 50 cm (62 x 20 in)

Instructions:
1. Cut a piece approximately 18 cm (7 in) wide off one end of each scarf or rectangle of fabric. This will be used to make the pockets. Finish both raw edges of the pocket pieces. If scarves with fringed ends are used, the fringe can be left on as decoration. This will eliminate the need to finish the bottom edge of the pocket piece.

2. Machine or hand sew the ends of the scarves or pieces of fabric together as shown in Diagram 1. This forms a double layer of fabric in the back.

3. Sew a pocket piece onto the free end of each scarf, leaving the top edge open. Rows of stitching may be used to divide the large pocket into pockets of a more convenient size (Diagram 2).

cm (4 in)   Diagram 1   Diagram 2

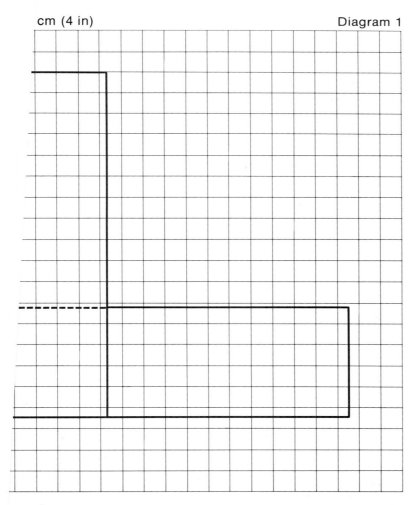 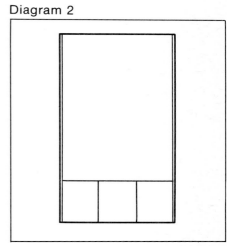

Poncho

A poncho may be worn to keep the shoulders and upper part of the body warm while sitting.

Materials:

mohair scarf, 160 x 50 cm (62 x 20 in)

Mohair is warm and yet very lightweight. A nylon and mohair blend is washable. Fabrics sold by the yard could also be used.

Instructions:

1. If using a scarf, fold it in half and cut along the fold so that you have two pieces of equal length. Raw edges usually do not have to be finished in mohair because the many tiny fibers stick together and prevent fraying. When using fabric by the meter (yard), cut two rectangles so that the finished size of each (when the raw edges are finished to prevent fraying) is approximately 80 x 50 cm (30 x 20 in).

2. Hand or machine stitch the two pieces together as shown in Diagram.

3. Sew the remaining ends together in the same manner (match A to A, and B to B). You now have a poncho that slips on over the head. By only sewing the front seam part way, a large neck opening can be fastened with press tape or a decorative frog can be created.

cm (2 in)

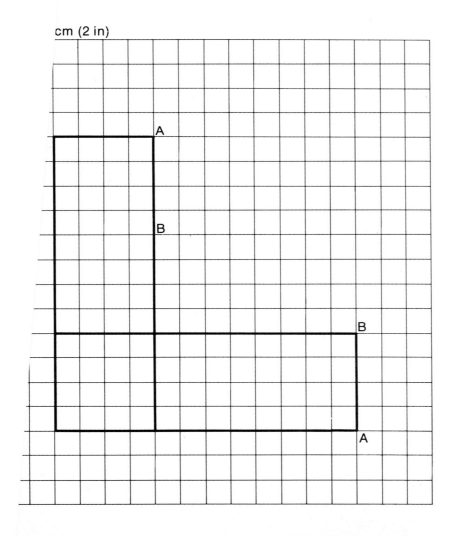

207

Belt and neck purses

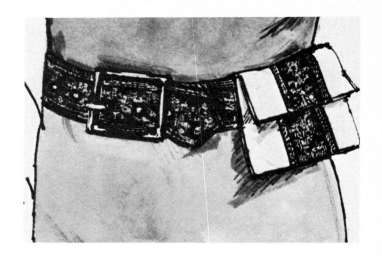

Handicapped people and elderly people often have problems in carrying eye glasses, pills, money, or other items with them at home as they go around their daily chores or when they go out to shop or visit. One answer to the problem is to have a purse which slips over any belt that you might be wearing. Anyone proficient at leatherwork could make them for a friend at a relatively low cost or they can be bought ready-made. They could also be made of fabric with interfacing. The man using crutches may find it inconvenient to fill pockets in trousers and coats since this weight and bulk may interfere with the use of the crutches. The separate purse which can be slipped over any belt could be used by men as well as by women and children.

208

kets

s of clothing, particularly
othing, do not have an adequate
ockets. Belt pockets are useful in
in be worn with any outfit.
ey hang loose when the person is
y are easier to reach into than
ary pockets. The top of the pockets
sed with Velcro or snaps to
e contents from spilling out. The
in be made with their own matching
slipped on to a purchased belt.

Type A

Materials:
0.20 m (¼ yd) fabric
decorative braid
Velcro

Instructions:
1. Cut two rectangles of fabric, 18 x 20 cm (7 x 8 in) for each pocket.

2. With right sides together, sew two pieces together around three sides, making an envelope with one side left open. Turn right side out and finish the top edge to prevent ravelling.

3. Loops to attach the pocket to a belt can be made from strips of fabric or decorative braid. For easiest access, sew the loop to the back of the pocket.

4. Snaps or Velcro can be attached to close the pocket top.

Type B

Materials:
0.45 m (½ yd) firm fabric, soft suede or leather
purchased belt or decorative braid to fit the
waist
1.50 m (1⅝ yd) decorative binding
25 cm (10 in) double-fold bias tape

Instructions:
1. For each pocket, cut one of A, B, and C.

2. Finish the top edge of A with double-fold
bias tape. Fold A along the dotted lines.
Fold so that the wrong sides of the fabric are
together. Press. Bring the folded edges
together so that they lay along the center
front line. Press. This forms an inverted
pleat which will extend to provide more room
in the pocket.

3. Place A and B with right sides together and
bottom edges matching. Stitch together,
leaving the top edge open. Turn and press.

4. C is the flap facing. Place it against the top
portion of B, right sides together. Stitch
from dot to dot around the curved portion.

5. Turn under the seam allowance on the
slanted portion of the side of the facing.
Secure the loose bottom edge of the facing to
the pocket back by hand or machine stitching
(D to E). You now have a casing with open
ends through which a narrow belt can pass.

6. A closure for the pocket top can be added
if desired.

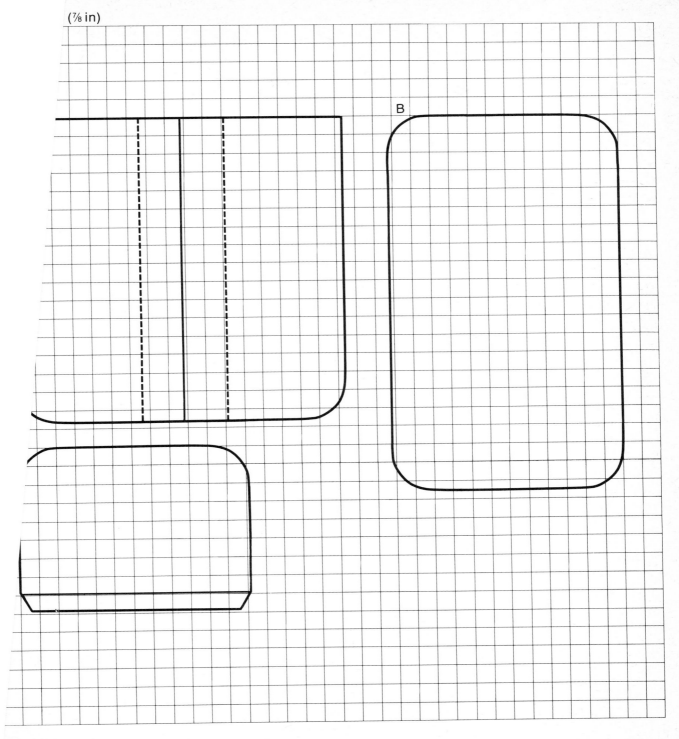

B

Type C   **Materials:**
0.45 m (½ yd) firm fabric
double-fold bias tape
purchased belt or decorative braid to fit the
waist measurement

Instructions:
1. For each pocket, cut one of A, B, and C.

2. On A and on B, crease along the dotted lines so that the wrong sides of the fabric are together.

3. Place A and B with right sides together, raw edges of sides together, and bottom edges matching. Stitch both sides. Turn.

4. With the pocket turned right side out, close the bottom so that the pressed-in folds will form pleats along the sides. These pleats will extend, making more room in the pocket. Finish the bottom with binding.

5. C is the flap facing. Place it against the top portion of B, matching the curved edges and with wrong sides together. Stitch from dot to dot, leaving the bottom edge open. Turn and press.

6. Finish the edge of the slanted portion of the side of the facing by zig-zagging or by turning under a tiny amount. Secure the loose bottom edge of the facing (D to E) to the pocket back by hand or machine. You now have a casing with open ends through which a narrow belt can pass.

7. Finish the raw edges of the pocket top and flap with binding.

8. A closure for the pocket top can be added if desired.

212

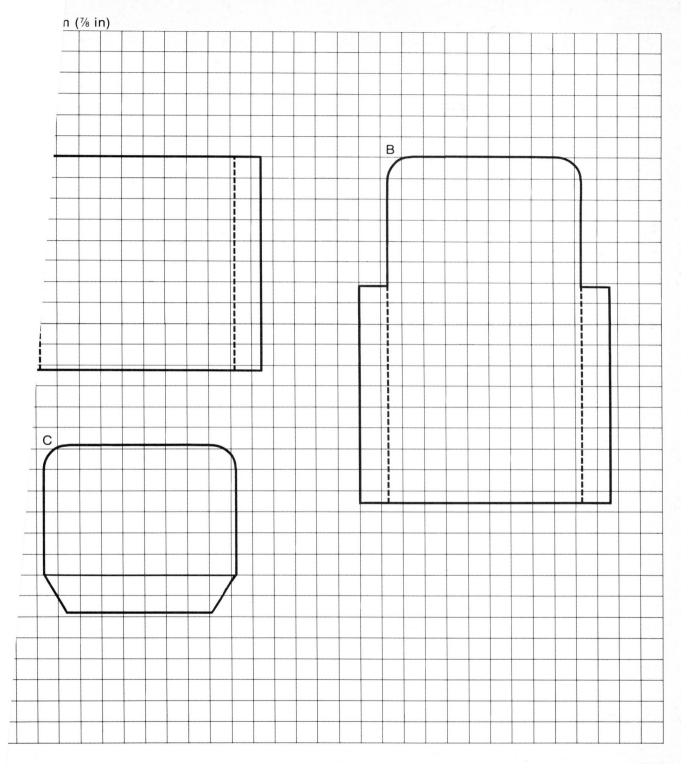

Type D

Materials:
0.45 m (½ yd) firm fabric
purchased belt or decorative braid to fit waist
0.20 m (¼ yd) fabric for contrasting pocket
1 m (1⅛ yd) trim
10 cm (4 in) Velcro

Instructions:
1. Cut one of A, B, C, and D for each pocket.

2. Finish the top edge of A.

3. On A, fold along the solid lines so that wrong sides of the fabric are together. Fold along the dotted lines so that right sides of the fabric are together. Press.

4. Finish the edges of D. Center on A. Stitch around three sides, leaving the top end open. This forms an extra pocket on top of the larger pocket. The small pocket may be trimmed.

5. C is the flap facing. Match it to the top portion of B with right sides of the fabric together. Stitch together, leaving the bottom edge open. Turn and press.

6. Place A and B with right sides together, raw edges together, and bottom edges matching. Stitch both sides.

7. Pin the bottom so that the pressed in folds will form pleats along the sides. Stitch across the bottom. These pleats will extend, making more room in the pocket. Turn pocket right side out.

8. Fold the long strip at the top of the pocket so that a portion of the end will overlap the pocket top. A closure can be attached at this point. Further up, sew across the strip to form a loop through which a belt can be put.

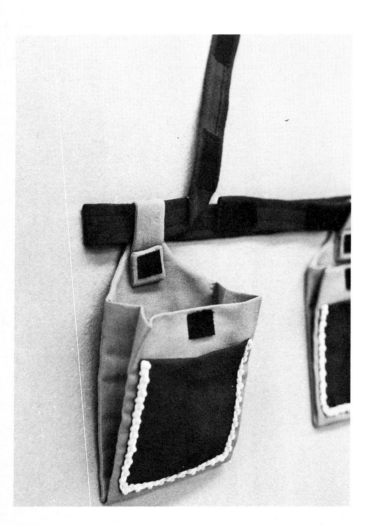

214

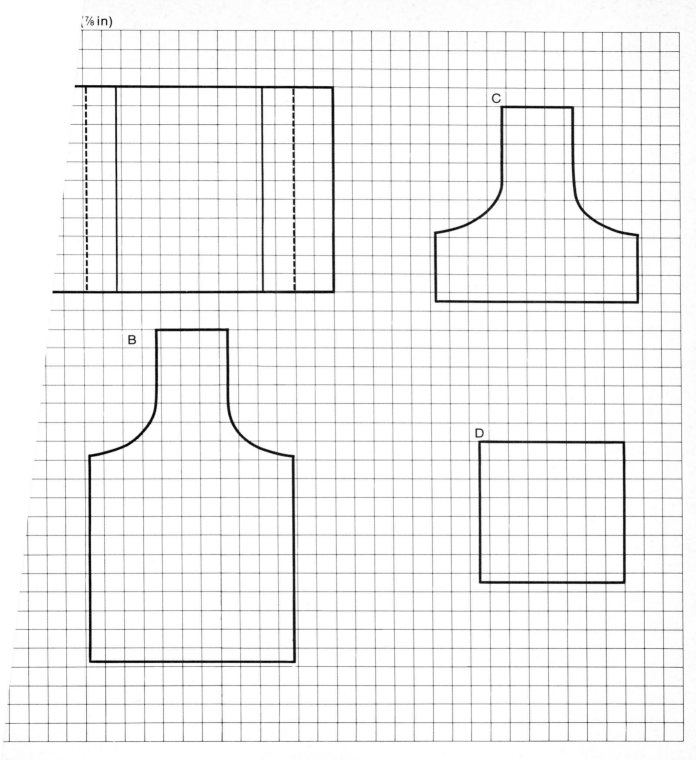

Walker carry-all

Materials:
0.70 m (¾ yd) firm fabric
25 cm (10 in) Velcro or other fastener

A carrier can be attached to a walker to make transporting articles much easier.

Instructions:

1. Cut two rectangles of fabric using the dimensions given in Diagrams A and B.

2. Mark lines for small pockets on one, and for large pockets on the other.

3. Cut strips of fabric for pockets, 1 strip for small pockets (Diagram D) and 1 strip for large pockets (Diagram C). Mark the center line of each pleat segment (dotted lines) on the fabric. Finish the top of the pocket strips by binding or hemming.

4. Match dotted lines on pockets to those on the rectangular pieces of fabric. Machine stitch together on these lines, fastening your stitching securely at both ends.

5. Put rectangular pieces with right sides together. Sew up the sides. Turn right side out. You now have a tube with open ends.

6. Sew the top together: zig-zag right side or turn tube inside out and sew a seam across the top or use binding.

7. Finish the bottom by hemming, or binding the circular opening.

8. Attach fastenings to form a casing which fastens over the bar of the walker. In the one shown a strip of Velcro has been attached, however, snaps may also be used.

(1¼ in)

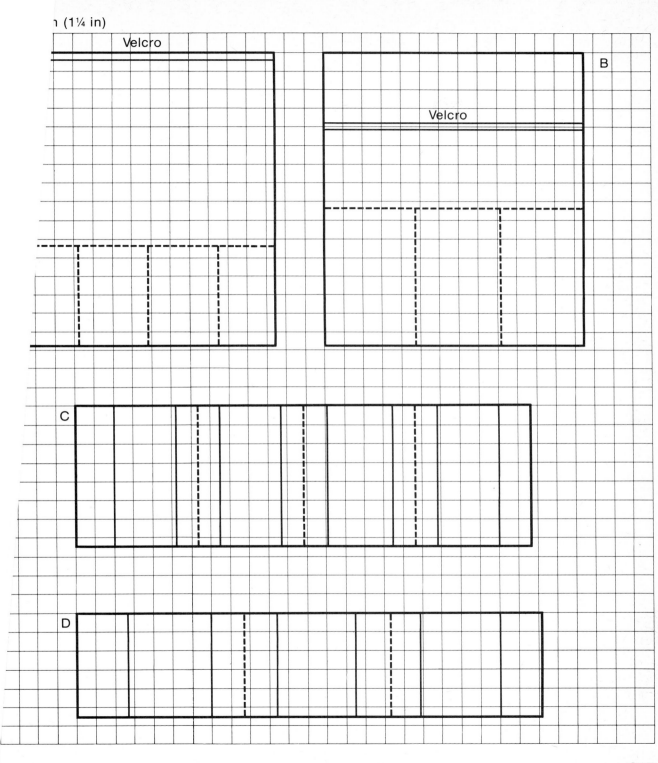

Velcro

B

Velcro

C

D

Knapsack bag

A knapsack with straps to fasten over the shoulders and around the waist is convenient for a person whose hands are occupied with crutches or a walker. The bag can be worn in front or back.

The pen shown hangs around the neck by means of leather thonging. Most ball point pens could be modified so that they too could be carried around the neck and be available whenever needed.

Carrying bag for wheelchair

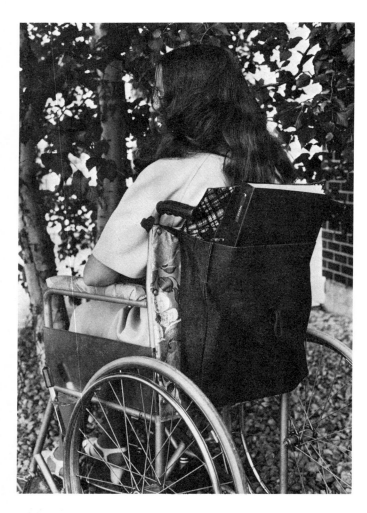

The bag measuring 35.5 x 35.5 cm (14 x 14 in) attaches across the handgrips on the back of the wheelchair. It can be used to carry books, groceries, and other items. It can be made from various fabrics—plain or trimmed, lined or unlined, depending on the intended use as well as the likes and dislikes of the individual concerned. A strap can be attached so that the bag can be converted to a back pack when not used on the wheelchair. Similarly small zippered pockets can be attached at the most convenient locations inside for carrying small items.

laid with the lengthwise grain of

  outer fabric
  suitable lining
  n (4 x 14 in) interfacing

laid with crosswise grain of

  d) fabric 90 cm (36 in) wide
  ıg
  m (4 x 14 in) interfacing

ɔns:
  ıterfacing to wrong side of bag
  ɔng GHJI. Stitch several rows of
  o stiffen bag bottom.

  ıp of bag sides folding along fold

  ght sides of fabric and lining stitch
  ɔm (½ in) seam allowance from A
  ɔ B, C and D reinforcing at A and D.
  ɨam at A and D. Trim seam allowance.

  right sides out. Press.

  ɾight sides together stitch sides to bag
  at E matching NE, MG, LH, KA.
  ɾr side likewise.

  seam allowance. Overcast or bind

  ı right sides out.

  ʹ small pocket on flap if desired.

  ɨach wheelchair handle ties at points A

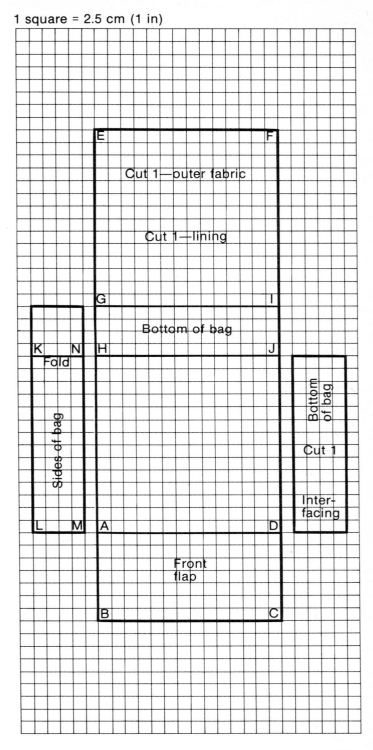

1 square = 2.5 cm (1 in)

E   F
Cut 1—outer fabric
Cut 1—lining
G   I
Bottom of bag
K   N   H   J
Fold
Sides of bag
Bottom of bag
Cut 1
Interfacing
L   M   A   D
Front flap
B   C

Wheelchair bag

A bag can be fastened over the arm of a wheelchair to make carrying small items easier.

Materials:
0.45 m (½ yd) of firm fabric
2 m (2¼ yd) binding
1.60 m (1¾ yd) of firmly woven tape or braid
3.8 cm (1½ in) wide to make straps to fit over the arm of the wheelchair
30 cm (12 in) zipper

Instructions:
1. Cut one each of A, B, C, and D. The same or contrasting fabric can be used for the different pieces.

2. Finish the raw edges of D by binding, making a narrow hem, or zig-zagging. Center it on B with the straight edge facing away from the dotted line.

3. Sew D onto B, leaving the straight edge open, to form a small pocket.

4. Match the dotted lines on A and B so that the right sides of piece B and section A2 are together.

5. Stitch along the dotted line and press the seam so that B is now laying against section A1.

6. Finish the top edge of B by binding or making a tiny hem.

7. Cut the piece of tape or braid which is to be used to make straps to fasten the bag to the arm of the wheelchair, into two pieces of equal length. (*Continued overleaf*)

(⅞ in)

1 square = 2 cm (⅞ in)

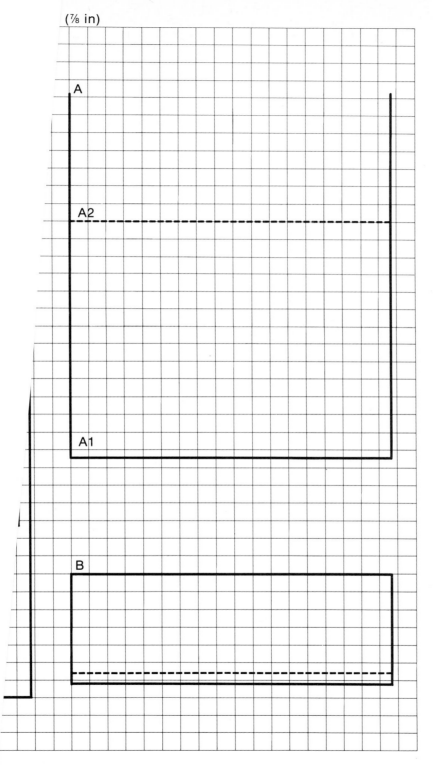

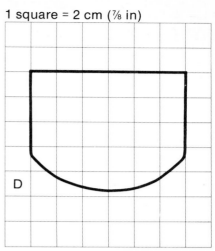

A

A2

A1

B

D

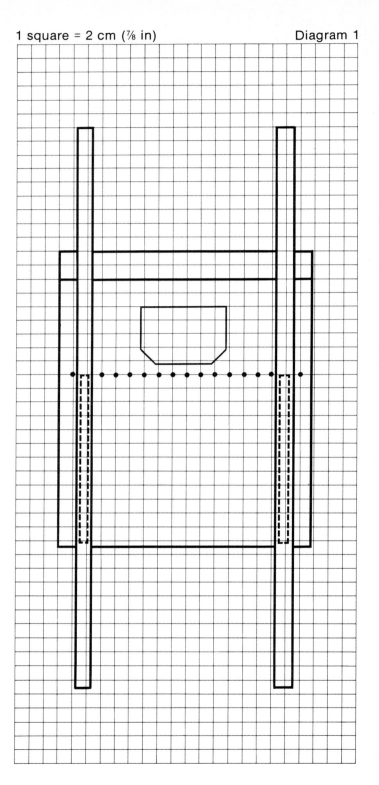

1 square = 2 cm (⅞ in)   Diagram 1

8. Position the straps as shown in Diagram 1 and stitch on the dotted lines to secure them to the fabric.

9. Center a 30 cm (12 in) zipper on C (see pattern piece) and zig-zag or top-stitch it in place. Cut away the narrow strip of fabric underneath the zipper.

10. Fold A, wrong sides together, on two lines which run perpendicular to the rows of tape or braid which will form straps. This will form the sides and bottom of the carry-all. See Diagram 2.

11. Fold C, and position it against A, wrong sides together, as shown in Diagram 2. Sew the two together with a 6 mm (¼ in) seam.

12. Finish raw edges with binding.

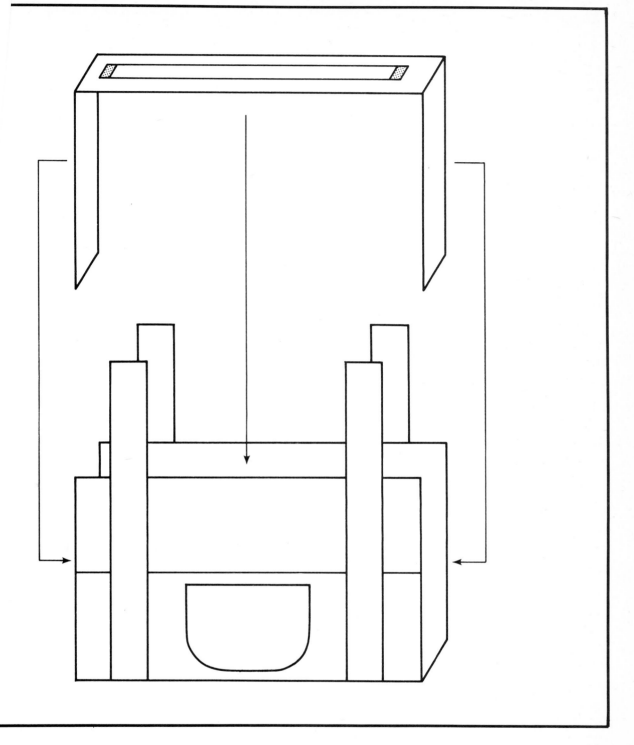

Aid for putting on socks

A sock aid is useful for those who cannot bend their legs and so have difficulty in putting on socks.

Materials:
paper about the weight of a file folder
masking tape
2 stocking garters
1.5 m (1⅝ yd) twill tape, 1.3 cm (½ in) wide

Instructions:
1. Cut the pattern from two layers of paper.

2. Bind the two layers together with masking tape around the edges.

3. Make a hole in each side, about 4 cm (1½ in) from top and 2.5 cm (1 in) from side as marked on the accompanying pattern. Reinforce with masking tape.

4. Fold around a cylindrical object such as a rolling pin. Tie in place and moisten. Allow to dry.

5. Cut 1 m (1⅛ yd) of twill tape. Attach a garter to each end.

6. Cut two 25 cm (10 in) pieces of twill tape. Thread one through each hole in the paper. Thread through hole again. Stitch one end of the tape to itself about 2.5 cm (1 in) above paper form. Stitch the other end of this tape to the tape end with the garter. Do the same for the other side.

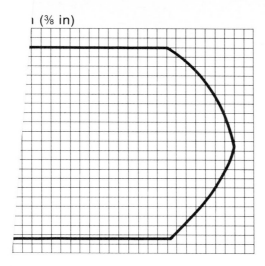

ı (⅜ in)

; for use

: rounded end of the form
y into the toe of the sock and pull
about half way up the form. Fasten
:r to each side of the sock.

:he form and sock to the floor,
ɔn to the tapes. Insert the foot into
. It may help to hold the form
ry with the other toe or a cane and
toe against a solid object like a wall.

ɔn the tapes to advance the sock up
ı and onto the leg. When the sock is in
ı, unfasten the garters and pull the
orm out of the sock.

Adaptation

A similar aid can be made without a form. A
piece of twill tape or braid 1 m (1⅛ yd) long is
needed. Stitch a garter to each end of this
tape. It is used in the same manner as
the form. When the sock is in position the
garters are unfastened.

Cast boot

A boot of soft, warm fabric will keep the exposed part of a foot and leg in a cast warm. The front zipper opening simplifies insertion of the foot and is convenient to reach.

Materials:
0.45 m (½ yd) soft warm fabric such as pile
40 cm (16 in) zipper

Instructions:
1. Stitch the lower center front seam of boot below where the zipper will end.

2. Press under 16 mm (⅝ in) seam allowances on the center front opening above the stitched portion.

3. Center the zipper in the center front opening, placing the folded edges about 6 mm (¼ in) back from the zipper teeth. Stitch around the zipper close to the folded edges. Be sure to stitch through the zipper tape.

4. Stitch center back seam of boot leg.

5. Fold upper edge of boot under 2.5 cm (1 in) and stitch.

6. With right sides together, stitch the boot leg to the boot sole using a 13 mm (½ in) seam allowance. Clip curves. Turn.

Note: A shorter zipper can be inserted and a decorative frog closing used at the top of the boot.

cm (1⅝ in)

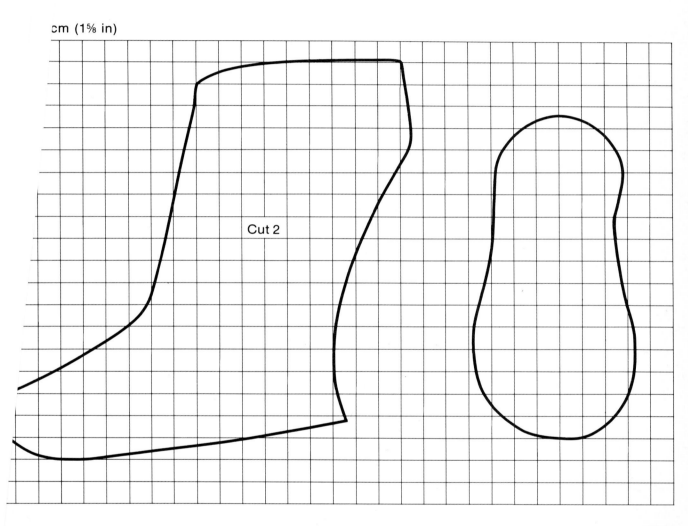

Cut 2

Boot slipper

Boot slippers are useful for keeping arthritic feet warm. The zipper down the back of the boot allows a bigger opening for inserting the foot. The encircling ankle strap helps to hold the boot on, especially when there is little feeling in the foot. The sole of the boot is padded for comfort and the under sole is leather to prevent slipping.

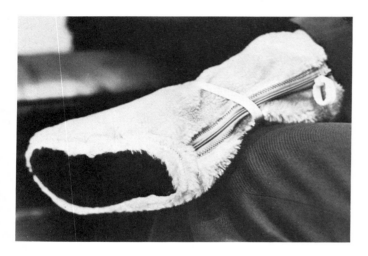

Materials:

30 cm (12 in) soft warm fabric such as pile fabric
30 cm (12 in) stretch binding
15 cm (6 in) leather or suede
22 cm (9 in) zipper
one 4 cm (1½ in) button

Instructions:

1. Cut two boot soles from the boot fabric, and one from the leather. Trim 2.5 cm (1 in) from edges of the leather sole and one of the fabric soles.

2. Place the zipper, right side up, on the center back of the boot leg. Stitch close to edges of zipper tape. Trim fabric underneath zipper close to the stitching.

3. Stitch front seam of boot leg. Stitch one end of the stretch binding into this seam, about 16 cm (6 in) down from the top of the boot.

4. Turn upper edge of boot under 2.5 cm (1 in) and stitch.

5. Place the two fabric soles, wrong sides together with the smaller one centered on the larger one. Center the leather sole on the other side of the full size fabric sole. Stitch around the edges of the smaller soles, stitching through the three layers of fabric.

e leg of the boot to the sole, right
er, using a 13 mm (½ in) seam
Be sure to stitch the end of the
in this seam.

e button to the center front seam,
(2 in) from the top. Form a loop in
the stretch binding to fit around
. A loop of the stretch binding can
d to the zipper pull tab to make
the zipper easier.

1 square = 4 cm (1⅝ in)

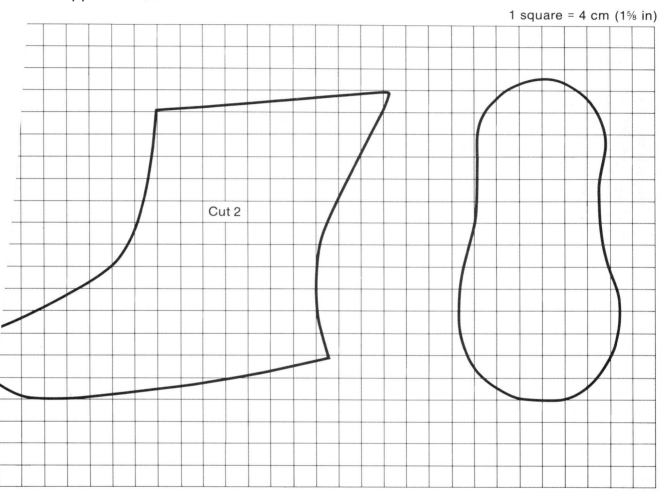

Cut 2

231

Toe cozy

A toe cozy is useful in keeping exposed toes warm when a walking cast or other leg cast is worn. The cozy is held on by elastic around the heel.

1 square = 0.5 cm (³⁄₁₆ in)

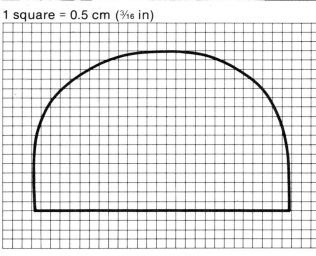

Materials:
0.15 m (⅛ yd) soft warm fabric
6 cm (2½ in) rib knit fabric
elastic sufficient to stretch around heel of cast

Instructions:
1. Cut two of the toe cozy patterns.

2. With right sides together, stitch the two pieces together along the curved edges. Use a 10 mm (⅜ in) seam allowance.

3. Cut a length of rib knit fabric to fit around the open edge of the toe cozy. Stitch the ends together to form a ring of fabric.

4. Fold rib knit in half, with raw edges together. Place it around the raw edge of the toe cozy, raw edges together. Stretch to fit. Stitch together, using a 6 mm (¼ in) seam allowance.

5. On one half of the toe cozy, center the elastic on the seam joining the rib knit to the cozy. The elastic should form a heel loop. Stitch the elastic securely to the seam allowance.

Socks with individual toe sections

These socks have been fashionable for some time and besides being fun to wear are particularly suitable for a parapalegic person who does not have the use of upper limbs. These socks enable the person to hold a tool between his toes and use his foot for writing, typing, painting, and so on.

air of shoes, originally fastened with a and buckle, has been converted with of Velcro stitched on by a shoemaker. ill make the closure easier to handle.

Leg warmers

Cylindrical men's socks

Footless socks would prove valuable for a person confined to a wheelchair and for anyone particularly sensitive to the cold. Aside from the warmth that they provide, leg warmers have the added advantage of being easily removed without having to take off shoes.

Leg warmers can be knitted to fit the wearer. The ones illustrated have 82 stitches cast on around the top with a K1, P1 ribbing of 19 cm (7½ in) wide at either end. The total length is 71 cm (28 in). Size of needles and number of stitches would vary with the weight of wool used.

Tubular socks are increasing in popularity in all men's departments. These are particularly suitable for a person with restricted movement since one does not have to put them on in any specific way.

Loops sewn at each side of the sock cuff facilitate putting on the socks with or without the use of a dressing stick.

Ice grippers

Separating cane with ice gripper

The cane, designed for use on ice, is available from Treasure Chest, Box 345, Montreal, H2V 4N2. Since it comes apart, it is easily carried when not in use.

Ice grippers may be worn over shoes or boots or over the tip of a cane or crutches. They are available from various sources including Rehabilitation Centres (see page 268). The purpose of ice grippers is to prevent a person from falling on ice. Ice grippers can be rubbed with wax before being used so that snow will not accumulate in them.

Arm sling

A sturdy, but comfortable arm sling can be made from a strip of firm belting 7 – 10 cm (3 – 4 in) in width. The sling is formed from a length of belting long enough for a 10 cm (4 in) loop to be formed at each end, and the belting to pass under the affected arm, across the back, and over the unaffected shoulder. The finished length of the sling is determined by the arm position most comfortable for the individual. The affected hand is placed in one loop of the belting and the loop moved up the forearm. The sling is then passed under the arm, around the back, and over the shoulder. The affected hand is placed in the second loop. This arrangement of the sling is necessary so that the weight of the arm is transferred to the unaffected shoulder.

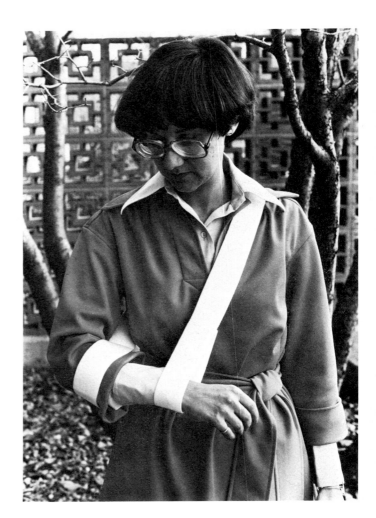

Mitten with side zipper closing

It is difficult to put mittens on an individual with limited finger and wrist mobility. A zipper inserted in the side of a mitten allows easy insertion and removal of the hand. It also insures correct finger placement in the mitten. A strip of fabric should be applied underneath the zipper to protect the wearer.

Materials:
mitten
20 cm (8 in) zipper

Instructions:
1. Place zipper on side of mitten without the thumb. Position so that the zipper opens at the wrist.

2. Stitch around zipper at edges of zipper tape, using a zig-zag stitch or several rows of straight stitching.

3. Slash mitten under zipper teeth. Slash only to the zipper stop. Trim fabric close to stitching.

Note: A zipper may also be inserted in the side seam of a hand-knitted mitten.

Wash mitt with soap pocket

This mitt is useful to those with limited finger and hand movement. The soap pocket allows good control of the soap bar.

Materials:
0.30 m (⅓ yd) terry toweling or small hand towel
8 cm (3 in) narrow elastic

Instructions:
1. Cut two mitt pieces and one soap pocket piece.

2. Stitch elastic to the top of the soap pocket. Turn under and stitch again, encasing elastic.

3. With right sides together, and soap pocket extending over the thumb area, stitch the pocket to the mitt from A to B as marked on the pattern.

4. Turn the soap pocket back over the mitt, matching curved edges. Lay second mitt on top so that pocket is in the middle. With right sides together sew around the mitt, stitching through all three layers of fabric.

5. Turn the mitt right side out. Press raw edge of wrist under and stitch in place.

1 square = 1 cm (⅜ in)

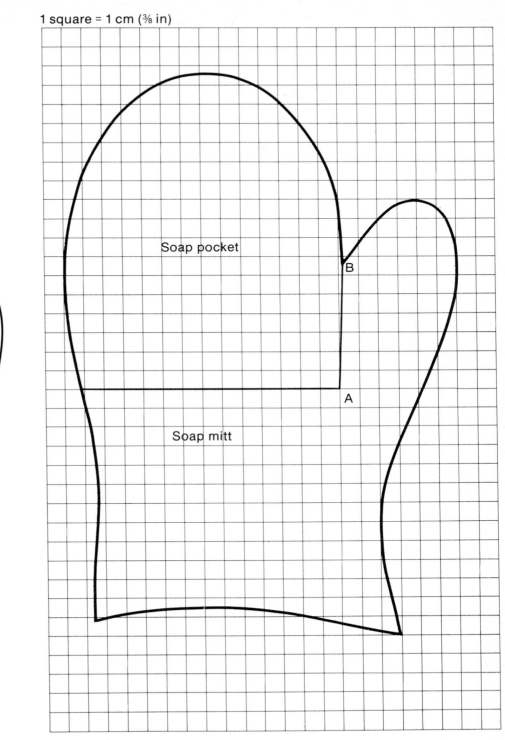

Soap pocket

B

A

Soap mitt

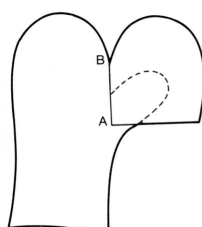

B

A

239

Oven mitt

A mitt that follows the natural position of the thumb and hand is more comfortable than one in which the thumb is spread.

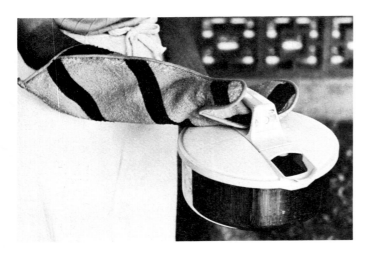

Materials:

0.30 m (⅓ yd) fabric for outer mitt
0.30 m (⅓ yd) fabric such as terry cloth for padding
1.30 m (1⅓ yd) double-fold bias tape

Instructions:

1. Draw mitt pattern to scale. Cut 1 of each pattern from outer fabric and one from padding.

2. Lay padding on wrong side of outer fabric and quilt by machine stitching the layers together over the surface of the mitt.

3. Lay quilted pieces together with right side of outer fabric outwards. Stitch together using 5 mm (¼ in) seam allowance.

4. Bind edges of mitt with bias tape.

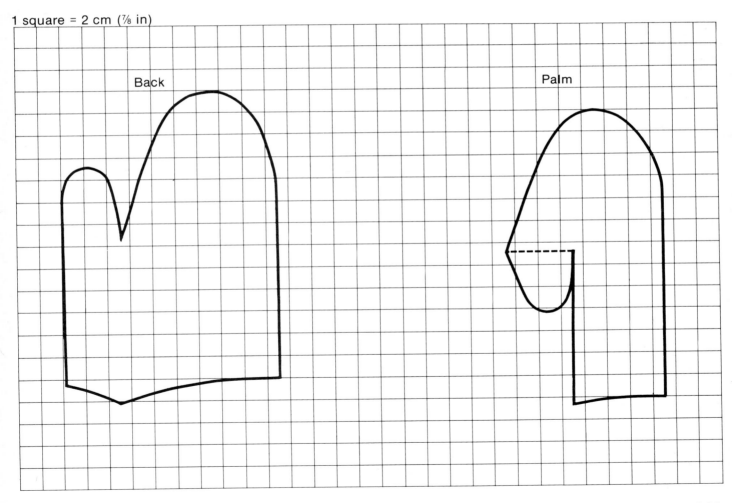

1 square = 2 cm (⅞ in)

Back

Palm

Wash bag

A person who lacks strength and dexterity in the hand may find it difficult to grip a facecloth. A wash bag which fastens with an adjustable belt over the hand will alleviate this problem.

Materials:
25 x 35 cm (10 x 14 in) piece of terry toweling
35 cm (14 in) twill tape 2.5 cm (1 in) wide
5 cm (2 in) Velcro
2 plastic rings

Instructions:
1. Hem one of the long edges of terry toweling AB with a 16 mm (⅝ in) seam.

2. With right sides together, fold terry cloth in half crosswise and stitch along the end ED to EC and the open side DA to CB of the bag. Turn bag right side out.

3. Stitch a plastic ring at one end of the twill tape.

4. Place the twill tape on the fold line parallel to the hemmed edge AB of the terry bag at F, approximately 2.5 cm (1 in) in from the edge. Stitch in place close to ring.

5. Put hand in bag and wrap twill tape around the wrist. Pass the free end of the tape through the first ring.

6. Remove mitt. Attach second ring at the free end of twill tape.

7. Stitch one strip of Velcro to upper side of twill tape close to the second plastic ring.

Velcro brush

8. With hand in bag, wrap twill tape around wrist to determine the location of the second piece of Velcro. Both strips of Velcro are on the same side of the twill tape. Stitch Velcro securely in place.

Note: After passing through the first ring, twill tape folds back on itself to fasten comfortably and keep the mitt from coming off. Tape is easily released by pulling on the second ring.

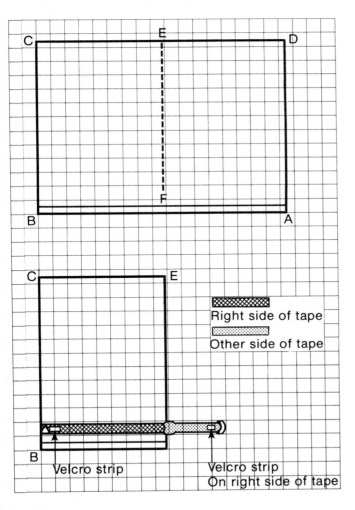

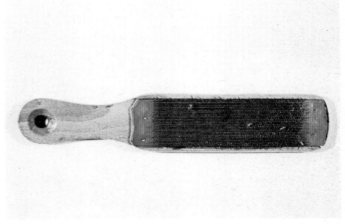

Velcro brushes are very similar to suede shoe brushes. While they are useful to remove lint that has collected on the hook side of Velcro, it has limited possibilities since it also tends to snag fabric which surrounds the Velcro.

Velcro should always be closed before washing to avoid lint from collecting. If it does collect, this Velcro brush or a regular suede shoe brush can be used but care must be exerted that snagging does not occur.

Wash sponge
with soap on handle

This sponge is commercially produced for the handicapped. The sponge slides on and off the handle and has a cavity into which a cake of soap can be inserted and then slipped on the handle.

Some long handle scrub sponges available on the market have a sponge permanently attached to the handle.

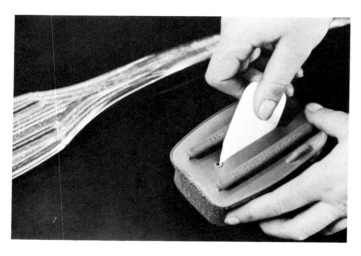

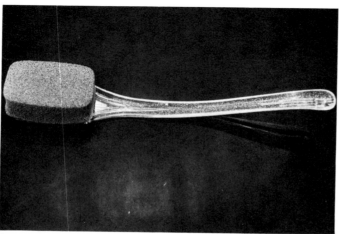

Sling towel

When a person has limited reaching ability, the back and other parts of the body are often difficult to dry. To aid in this task, tape loops may be sewn to each end of the towel, allowing the towel to be used as a sling.

Materials:
56 cm (22 in) twill tape
towel, approximately 95 x 50 cm (38 x 20 in)

Instructions:
1. Fold towel in half lengthwise, and stitch the long side together.

2. Cut twill tape into two pieces 28 cm (11 in) long.

3. Position twill tape with one end at each corner, forming a loop at each end. Stitch securely in place.

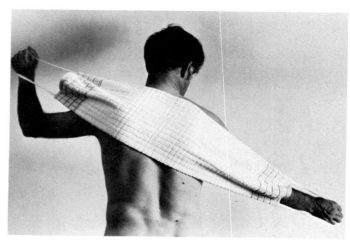

Belt with Velcro fastening

If a belt is desired but a belt buckle is difficult to handle due to limited finger dexterity, the belt can be changed to fasten with Velcro.

Materials:
belt with buckle
8 cm (3 in) Velcro

Instructions:
For purposes of discussion, the belt will be referred to as shown in the diagram.

1. Fasten belt so it fits comfortably around waist. Mark this position.

2. Remove buckle from belt.

3. Stitch Velcro strip to wrong side of belt at the open end of belt.

4. Slip buckle on, putting the buckle prong through both the belt and Velcro.

5. Stitch other piece of Velcro strip to the right side of belt at the opposite end or the end where the buckle is usually placed.

6. Fasten by pressing Velcro together.

Men's ties

The person with restricted arm and hand movement is not able to knot a tie. Yet, despite the trend away from wearing ties, there may be occasions when such a person would want to wear a shirt and tie.

One illustration shows the clip-on bow tie which may answer the problem. The other illustration shows the hook-on type of tie which is easily clipped to the shirt collar and easily removed. Both types are readily available in men's stores.

Velcro fastened ascot tie

Instant collar extender

These are commercially available aids which can add to the comfort of a shirt since it adds a full half size to a too tight collar. They are reusable, transferable, and invisible behind a tie. The loop slips over existing buttons, then the shirt can be buttoned up with ease.

Various styles of ties can be made or ready-made ones can be altered so that they either hook on to the shirt collar or fasten with Velcro.

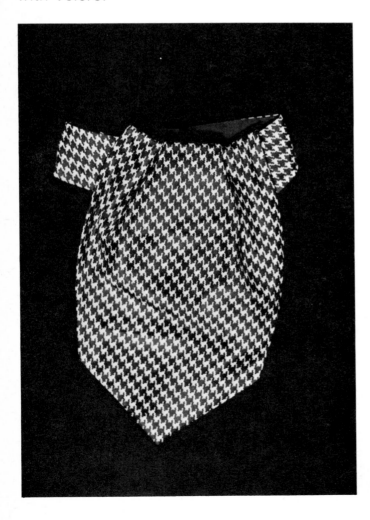

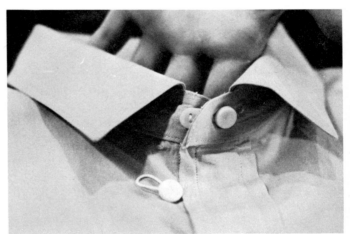

Zipper pull

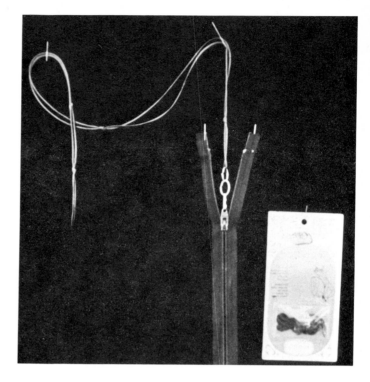

Zipper pulls are available commercially but may be made using a piece of cord approximately 117 cm long (46 in) and a safety pin. Pass the string through the circle at the closed end of the pin so that the string is halfway through. Tie a knot in the cord close to the pin to hold it in place and at the opposite end to keep both ends of the cord together.

In some cases it may be preferable to use a metal hook rather than a pin, since a hook would be easier to remove. Some drapery hooks can be modified successfully for this purpose.

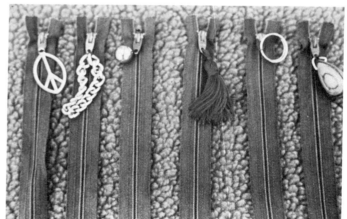

Long handle shoe horn

The long handle shoe horn makes the putting on of shoes easier for those who have problems in bending. They are available in most department stores.

Reaching and dressing sticks

One of the most essential tools for a person who has problems in bending is a gadget for reaching or grasping. The illustration shows a pair of barbecue tongs used for picking up anything that is otherwise out of reach.

Shown is an ordinary piece of wood dowel cut the desired length. A cup hook is inserted at one end. If desired, a different size hook may be inserted at the opposite end. Such a stick is an ideal gift for a friend who has a leg in a cast and therefore cannot bend the knee. This stick can be used as a dressing aid to pull on socks, underwear, and trousers.

A still simpler reaching tool is an ordinary wire clothes hanger pulled into a long loop with the hook at one end.

Cutlery

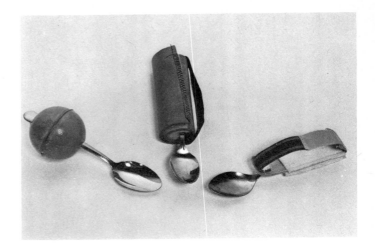

The illustration shows three types of adaptations to cutlery which would make them easier to handle if a person had restricted arm, wrist, and hand movement.

One spoon shown has a small rubber ball slipped over the handle. This gives a firmer grip on the spoon.

The fork and knife have bicycle handles slipped over the handle. Plaster of Paris is poured in the handle to firmly hold the knife and fork in place. These tools are heavy and are particularly useful for spastics.

Another spoon shown has a piece of foam rubber wound around the handle, then a piece of leather holds the foam rubber in place. In addition there is a ribbon which slips over the back of the hand. This is relatively light. The advantage is that with the band over the hand, the spoon does not fall, should there be unco-ordination of movements.

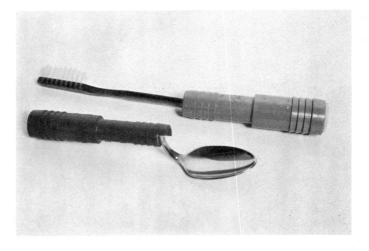

The final spoon is a commercially produced spoon with a bent handle swiveling in a plastic holder.

Wheelchair cover

Wheelchairs are usually covered with vinyl which does not absorb body moisture; thus it feels hot in warm weather and cold in cool weather. A comfortable wheelchair cover can be made from a towel.

Materials:
towel, 100 x 60 cm (40 x 24 in)
3.20 m (3½ yd) of 3 cm (1¼ in) twill tape
3 gripper snaps

Instructions:
1. Fold towel in half widthwise, right sides together. Stitch 2 cm (¾ in) from the foldline to form a casing.

2. Cut twill tape into three equal lengths. Fold one piece of tape so that it is half the original width, and stitch together. Thread this piece through the casing, and stitch the tape to the towel.

3. Stitch one piece of twill tape to the wrong side of the towel at each end along the entire width.

4. Lay towel, right side up on the wheelchair. Tie the middle tape behind the chair. Position gripper snaps to ends of upper and lower tape and ends of towel, to hold towel in place on chair. (May also be used on ordinary chairs.)

Card holder

A person with restricted hand movement may find holding cards impossible. These two devices are satisfactory substitutes.

1. A small box opened with the cover slipped over the bottom of the box, provides a groove for holding cards in an upright position. Such a holder is cost free, light, and can be used as a box when not used for this purpose.

2. A block of wood 25.5 cm (10 in) long, 9 cm (3½ in) wide and 3.8 cm (1½ in) thick may be made into a card holder by sawing two parallel grooves along the length of the block. The front groove which is about 2 cm (¾ in) from the front edge should be about 2.5 cm (1 in) deep and on an angle so the cards will slant slightly backwards. The back groove should be about 1.5 cm (⅝ in) in depth and at the same angle as the front groove. This will permit the back cards to be slightly higher and consequently more visible than if they were all on the same level. The card holder can be sandpapered thoroughly.
A good coat of wax should prove sufficient to protect the wood. A layer of felt may be glued to the bottom for a more finished appearance.

Wooden toys

There is a growing concern about the safety, the educational value, the durability, and the cost of children's toys. The ones illustrated have movable parts and are made from wood, assembled with wood dowelling. Some come apart and can be reassembled by the child. The finished toys are sandpapered but nothing is added such as paint, metal, pins, or nails which the child could pull off and put in his mouth. The toys illustrated are handcrafted by Bill Birse, Edmonton and sold at Harvest House Art Gallery.

R. J. Masters Marketing Co., 1435 – 26A Street, S.W., Calgary, Alberta, or Box 7127, Postal Station E, Calgary, Alberta, retails toys for all children but specifically for physically and mentally handicapped children. Educational toys of this nature are also being produced by others across Canada.

Wooden jigsaw puzzle

This is an ideal toy for a young child since it helps to develop manual dexterity and concept formation. It is entirely safe for the child to use and inexpensive to construct.

Materials:

piece of wood 2.5 cm (1 in) thick, 19 cm (7½ in) diameter

Instructions:

The slab of wood illustrated is cut in any interesting pattern. Each piece is carefully sandpapered so all edges are smooth and sliver free. Paint and wax are not applied since they may contain toxic materials which would be given off if the child puts the pieces of wood in his mouth.

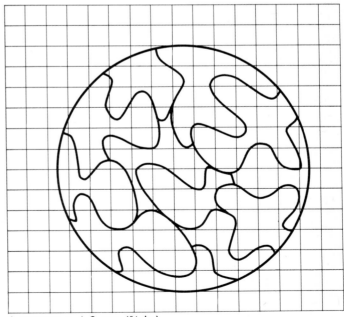

1 square = 1.6 cm (⅝ in)

Stuffed toys

These toys would be ideal for any child. They are designed to provide the child with opportunities for learning to button and unbutton, to fasten shoe laces, and to pull up and open a zipper. In addition, the toys can provide opportunities for developing color, size, and shape perception. The fabrics used can provide a variety of tactile sensations. The pillows are filled with polyester fiberfill, are completely machine washable and can be tumble dried.

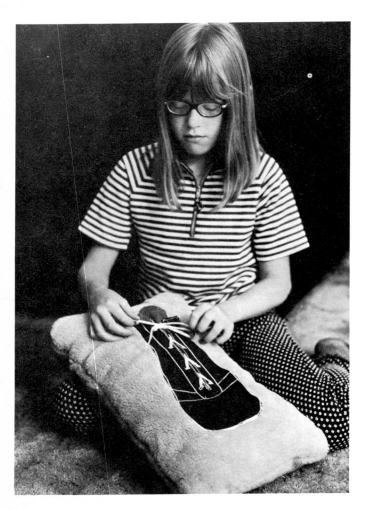

Puppets

These puppets can be easily designed and constructed from odd pieces of wool yarn or they can be sewn from scraps of fabric. The advantage of these toys is that there are no detachable notions added that can be pulled off by a child and swallowed. The puppets shown are made from crochet yarn and represent a panda bear and a snake.

Puppets may be used as toys in which case they encourage and promote the development of manual dexterity as well as the imagination of any child. For adults, they can be used profitably for exercise of fingers and wrists and as such, may prove valuable to a person with arthritic hands.

Source information

Research on clothing for special needs

Elderly

Allen, C. J. *Clothing design for the physically handicapped elderly woman.* Unpublished master's thesis, Montana State University, 1975.

Bader, I. *An exploratory study of clothing problems and attitudes of a group of older women.* Unpublished master's thesis, University of Iowa, 1962.

Bratcher, C. S. *Factors affecting clothing utilization of elderly women.* Unpublished master's thesis, Oklahoma State University, 1975.

Burnett, M. *Some socio-economic factors associated with clothing purchasing habits of a selected group of women sixty years of age and over.* Unpublished master's thesis, Oregon State University, 1964.

Frazier, C. A. *Clothing sizing: standards, ready-to-wear and body measurements for a selected group of women over sixty-two.* Unpublished master's thesis, Ohio State University, 1975.

Grey, N. C. *Some characteristics associated with the "most liked" and "least liked" outer garments in the wardrobes of people age sixty-five and over.* Unpublished master's thesis, Kansas State University, 1968.

Hargett, L. *A survey of problems pertaining to buying a ready-to-wear dress as expressed by a select group of women sixty-five years of age and over.* Unpublished master's thesis, University of Tennessee, 1963.

Hoffman, A. M. "Clothing behavioral factors for a specific group of women related to aesthetic sensitivity and certain socio-economic and psychological background factors," Ph.D. dissertation, Pennsylvania State University, 1956.

Jones, I. A. *An investigation to determine the relationship of clothing needs to the physiological, social, and psychological needs of the elderly in University City, Missouri.* Unpublished master's thesis, University of Missouri, 1975.

Malechek, K. R. *Body image as related to anxiety and fabric preference of aged women.* Unpublished master's thesis, Utah State University, 1974.

Massey, F. *Clothing needs of women over sixty-five years of age.* Unpublished master's thesis, University of North Carolina, 1964.

Miller, M. M. *Clothing behavior of a group of women living in a retirement home.* Unpublished master's thesis, University of Iowa, 1968.

Phillips, R. T. *Clothing as related to the social interaction and social class of older women.* Unpublished master's thesis, University of Kentucky, 1968.

Pieper, A. U. *Clothing needs of women sixty-five and older Stark County, Ohio.* Unpublished master's thesis, Kent State University, 1968.

Richards, J. M. *A study of the clothing needs and preferences of a selected group of women sixty years of age and over and their problems in shopping for suitable clothing.* Unpublished master's thesis, University of Maryland, 1971.

Richardson, P. C. *Clothing preferences and problems of a selected group of women sixty-five years of age* and over living in Tallahassee, Florida. Unpublished master's thesis, Florida State University, 1975.

Schuster, J. M. *Preferred style features in dresses for physically handicapped, elderly women.* Unpublished master's thesis, Oklahoma State University, 1973.

Shipley, S. *A comparative study of older women's preferences in clothing and the selection provided in the retail market.* Unpublished master's thesis, Michigan State University, 1961.

Skinner, S. D. *Color awareness, color preference, and color use in clothing for a selected group of elderly women.* Unpublished master's thesis, Ohio State University, 1975.

Smathers, D. G. *The effects of physical bodily changes caused by the natural aging process on clothing preferences of elderly women.* Unpublished master's thesis, University of Kentucky, 1974.

Walker, E. R. *Clothing preferences and purchasing concepts of older women and retail clothing buyers.* Unpublished master's thesis, Texas Woman's University, 1972.

Watson, M. G. *Daytime clothing interests and preferences of two groups of women sixty-five years and over.* Unpublished master's thesis, Iowa State University, 1965.

Children

Cannon, M. L. *Relationship of clothing and social activities of physically handicapped and non-handicapped children of junior high school age.* Unpublished master's thesis, University of Iowa, 1969.

Johnson, J. E. *Play garments for disabled children.* Unpublished master's thesis, Colorado State University, 1972.

Jordan, C. L. *Some garment design attributes that that contribute to parental satisfaction and dissatisfaction in clothing the physically handicapped child.* Unpublished master's thesis, Kansas State University, 1971.

Reeves, M. *Woven stretch and non-stretch fabrics in clothing designed for boys with specified physical handicaps.* Unpublished master's thesis, Oregon State University, 1966.

Siefert, E. R. *Physiological and psychological reactions to a developmental technique to teach self-help skills to the physically disabled child.* Unpublished master's thesis, University of Rhode Island, 1972.

Smiley, C. H. *Clothing perceptions of early adolescent girls with physical normalities and orthopedic physical disabilities.* Unpublished master's thesis, University of Maryland, 1971.

Taylor, L. P. *Dresses and a coat for physically handicapped girls, ages five through twelve, who use braces, crutches, and wheelchair.* Unpublished master's thesis, West Virginia University, 1963.

Arthritis

Madsen, J.K. *Adaptations of daytime dresses for women with rheumatoid arthritis.* Unpublished master's thesis, Purdue University, 1967.

Wolfson, S.R. *A study of the clothing needs of arthritic women.* Unpublished master's thesis, University of Maryland, 1969.

Cerebral palsy

Blair, A.R. *Instructional guide for cerebral palsied children: clothing fasteners related to articulation of upper extremities.* Unpublished master's thesis, Florida State University, 1975.

Dallas, M.J. *Daytime dresses for teenage girls and young adults with cerebral palsy.* Unpublished master's thesis, Colorado State University, 1965.

McGuire, L.M. *The design and evaluation of selected garments for the cerebral palsied female child.* Unpublished master's thesis, University of Oklahoma, 1970.

Sullivan, M.B. *Specific alterations of commercial patterns for a selected girl and spina bifida.* Unpublished master's thesis, Kansas State University, 1972.

Zaccagnini, J. *Adaptive fasteners of ready-to-wear knit pullover shirts for children with cerebral palsy.* Unpublished master's thesis, Kansas State University, 1970.

Mentally handicapped

Coolidge, J.L. *The relationship between self-help clothing features and independence in dress among moderately and severely retarded boys.* Unpublished master's thesis, Florida State University, 1974.

Frankenfield, J.L. *Clothing awareness of selected mentally handicapped high school girls in Davenport, Iowa.* Unpublished master's thesis, Iowa State University, 1970.

Olson, T.C. *Clothing for the institutionalized severely and profoundly mentally retarded.* Unpublished master's thesis, University of Wisconsin—Stout, 1973.

Peterson, T.C. *A comparison of schizophrenics, non-schizophrenics psychiatric patients and a normal group on body image, sensory perception and color.* Unpublished master's thesis, Utah State University, 1973.

Braces, crutches, wheelchair

Beck, B. K. *The psychological problems of adolescent girls wearing Milwaukee braces.* Unpublished master's thesis, University of Iowa, 1973.

Dedmon, K. A. *Techniques for adapting selected ready-to-wear and commercial patterns for the physically handicapped wearing Milwaukee braces.* Unpublished master's thesis, Florida State University, 1974.

Ewald, C. M. *Clothing needs of men with a physical disability wearing braces or artificial limbs.* Unpublished master's thesis, University of Arizona, 1975.

Rice, V. K. *Attractive garment designs for physically handicapped women who wear leg braces and who use crutches.* Unpublished master's thesis, Florida State University, 1971.

Richardson, N. J. *Dramatic play and dramatic play clothing for preschool physically handicapped boys wearing leg braces.* Unpublished master's thesis, University of Maryland, 1971.

Taylor, L. P. *Dresses and a coat for physically handicapped girls, ages five through twelve, who use braces, crutches, and wheelchair.* Unpublished master's thesis, West Virginia University, 1963.

Visually handicapped

Bissell, L. M. *A comparison of the interest, importance, and psychological aspects of clothing between a group of blind and sighted teenage girls.* Unpublished master's thesis, University of North Carolina, 1969.

Bryant, R. *An investigation of the methods used to teach clothing construction to the visually handicapped.* Unpublished master's thesis, University of Wisconsin—Stout, 1974.

Settle, J. H. *Relationships between body concept and clothing attitudes of blind and visually handicapped adolescents.* Unpublished master's thesis, Virgina Polytechnic Institute and State University, 1974.

Other

Bright, B. W. *A survey study of therapist's use and concepts of functional clothing in the rehabilitation process in four metropolitan areas of Tennessee.* Unpublished master's thesis, University of Tennessee, 1974.

Caddel, K. and S. Tank. "Specially designed clothing for a congenital quadruple amputee." Videotape, Natural Fibers and Food Protein Commission of Texas, Textile Research Centre, Texas Tech. University, School of Medicine, September 15, 1977.

Honea, P. L. *Clothing preferences and emotional adjustment in mastectomized women.* Unpublished master's thesis, Texas Tech University, 1974.

Sindelar, M. B. *Clothing satisfactions and preferences of physically disabled homemakers.* Unpublished master's thesis, University of Nebraska, 1969.

Williams, S. A. *Clothing problems and dissatisfactions of physically handicapped men.* Unpublished master's thesis, Oklahoma State University, 1975.

Books

Bare, C., E. Boettke, & N. Waggoner, *Self-help clothing for handicapped children*. Chicago: National Society for Crippled Children and Adults, 1962.

Caddel, K. *Measurements, guidelines and solutions*. Lubbock, Texas: Vintage Press, 1977.

Gifford, L. *If you can't stand to cook; easy-to-fix recipes for the handicapped homemaker*. Grand Rapids, Michigan: Zendervan Corp., 1973.

May, E. E., N. R. Waggoner, & E. M. Boettke, *Homemaking for the handicapped*. New York: Dodd, Mead & Company, 1966.

May, E. E., N. R. Waggoner, & E. B. Hotte, *Independent living for the handicapped and the elderly*. Boston: Houghton Mifflin Company, 1974.

McMichael, J. K. *Handicap. A study of physically handicapped children and their families*. London: Staples Press, 1971.

Nichols, P. J. R. *Rehabilitation of the severely disabled 2-management*. London: Butterworth and Company Ltd., 1971.

Pamphlets

A handicapped child in your home. U.S. Department of Health, Education, and Welfare; Office of Child Development. [DHEW Publication No. (OCD) 73–29]. Washington, D.C.: U.S. Government Printing Office, 1973.

Aid: A directory of community services for Edmonton and district. Edmonton: Aid Service of Edmonton, 1974, 1977.

Deck, H. L. *Group treatment for parents of handicapped children*. U.S. Department of Health, Education, and Welfare. [DHEW Publication No. (HSM) 73–5503]. Washington, D.C.: U.S. Government Printing Office.

Browning, R. W., Rupert, L. B., & Arner, L. B. (Eds.). *Proceedings of the workshop developing independent living skills for the physically handicapped*. Pennsylvania: School of Home Economics, Indiana University of Pennsylvania, 1974.

Caddel, K. *The natural creations*. Lubbock, Texas: Textile Research Centre, Texas University.

Clothing fastenings for the handicapped and disabled. London: Disabled Living Foundation, No date.

Clothing for long-stay patients. Supplements A, B, C, D, & E. (Shirley Institute Report Reference No. 21/13/138). Manchester: The Cotton, Silk, and Man-made Fibers Research Association, Shirley Institute, 1970.

Comfortable clothes (2nd ed.). Manchester: Shirley Institute, 1974.

Convenience clothing and closures. New York: Talon/
Velcro Consumer Education.

Davis, Wendy. *Aids to make you able.* Prairie Division
M.S. Society of Canada, 1977.

Elphick, L. *Incontinence, some problems, suggestions,
and conclusions.* London: Disabled Living
Foundation, 1970.

England, M. D. *Footwear for problem feet.* London:
Disabled Living Foundation, 1973.

*Flexible Fashions: clothing tips and ideas for the
woman with arthritis.* Supplier of Documents, U.S.
Government Printing Office, Washington, D.C.,
20402, U.S.A.

Forbes, G. *Clothing for the handicapped child.*
London: Disabled Living Foundation, 1971.

Gamweil, A. M., Joyce F. *A survey of problems of
clothing for the sick and disabled.* London: The
Disabled Living Activities Group, 1966.

*Guide for the dependent handicapped; a directory of
services in Edmonton, Alberta.* Alberta Association
for the Dependent Handicapped, Box 1846,
Edmonton, Alberta.

Hinshaw, E. S. & Barrier, D. L. *Physically handicapped:
aids to self help in homemaking, grooming and
clothing.* North Carolina: North Carolina
Agricultural Extension Service.

Lord, J. *Clothing for the handicapped and disabled in
hospital or in the community, a review of world
literature 1937-1970.* (Shirley Institute Report Ref.
No. 21/13/138). Manchester: Shirley Institute, 1970.

Macartney, P. *Clothes sense for handicapped adults of
all ages.* London: the Disabled Living Foundation,
1973.

Nutrition: a national priority. A report by Nutrition
Canada to the Department of National Health and
Welfare. Catalogue No. H58-26/1973. Ottawa:
Information Canada, 1973.

Srot, G. M. *Teaching a handicapped child to dress.*
Friends of the Center for Spastic Children, 63
Cheyne Walk, London, England, SW3 5NA.

Yep, J. *Clothes to fit your needs.* Iowa: Cooperative
Extension Service, Iowa State University, 1974.

Articles

Dahlman, S., M. Karrholm & E. Rosenblad-Wallin,
"Hygiene and clothing problems for elderly people—
areas in need of technological development,"
Journal of Consumer Studies and Home Economics,
1, 1977, pp. 73– 85.

Ebeling, M. and M. L. Rosencranz, "Social aspects of
clothing for older women," *Journal of Home
Economics*, LIII, No. 6 (June 1961), pp. 464–465.

People helping people—clothing and aids. Vocational
Guidance and Rehabilitation Services, 2239 East
55th St., Cleveland, Ohio, 44103.

Catalogues

Galt Early Stages. Distributed by R. J. Masters
Marketing Co. Ltd., 1435 - 26A Street S.W., P.O. Box
7127 - Stn. E., Calgary, Alberta, T3C 3L8.

Disabled Living Foundation Information Service,
Publication List, 346 Kensington High Street,
London, W14 8NS.

Mid-Canada Medical, Rehabilitation Specialties.
Mid-Canada Medical, 1236 Albert Street, Regina,
Saskatchewan.

Velcro ideas. Canadian Velcro Ltd., 5200 Dixie Road,
Suite 202, Mississauga, Ontario, L4W 1E4.

Aids for handicapped. Fred Sammons, Inc., Box 32,
Brookfield, Illinois, 60513.

Specialist suppliers

1. Extra-long zippers may frequently be obtained from upholstery or tent and awning manufacturers. Talon-Lightning will manufacture individual zippers to order.

Talon-Lightning Fastener
Textron Division
St. Catharines, Ontario
Canada.

Various styles and sizes of zippers are retailed by:

Dressmakers' Supply
1325 Bay Street
Toronto, Canada
M5R 2C5

2. Velcro information may be obtained from:

Canadian Velcro Ltd.   Talon Consumer Education
5200 Dixie Road   41 East 51 Street
Suite 202   New York, N.Y. 10022
Mississauga, Ontario
L4W 1E5

3. Lingerie shops frequently stock specialized clothing such as bras and swimwear for the woman who has had a mastectomy, and robes with lapped back openings for the bedridden, chairbound, or incontinent person. One such store is:

Edith Foran Shops
10062 – 104 Street
Edmonton, Alberta
T5J 0Z8

4. Mail order catalogues often supply small pieces of equipment such as ice grippers, separating canes, cane with ice gripper tip, and iron-on Velcro. One such source is:

Treasure Chest Ltd.
Rush Order Department
P.O. Box 345
Montreal, Quebec
H2V 4N2

Ice grippers for shoes or canes can also be obtained from:

Edmonton Rehabilitation Centre
10215 – 112 Street
Edmonton, Alberta T5K 1M7

5. Appliance covers for ileostomy, colostomy, or urostomy appliances are available. They increase comfort by providing a fabric layer between the skin and the appliance. One mail-order source of such appliances is:

Sarah Soft Wear
Route 1
Red Wing, Minnesota, 55066
Phone: 612—388-3104

6. Custom made clothes and aids are available for the handicapped individual. Each garment is designed to meet the needs of the disabled, in style, size, and function. Some firms offering such a service are:

Clothing Adjustment Service
488 Madison Avenue
Calumet City, Illinois
60409
Phone: 312—862-2614

Vocational Guidance and Rehabilitation Services
2239 East 55th Street
Cleveland, Ohio
44103

Fashion Able
Rocky Hill, New Jersey
08553

Leinenweber Custom Tailored Wheelchair Garments
69 West Washington Street
Chicago, Illinois
60602

7. Other organizations provide do-it-yourself instructions so that ready-to-wear garments can be adjusted or altered, according to the individual's disabilities. Further information may be obtained from:

William Schey
Designer of Specialized Clothing
c/o DYS Squire Apparel Co.
Apparel for Special Needs
488 Madison Avenue
Calumet City, Illinois
60409
Phone: 312—682-2614

Fashions by Levi
c/o Clothing Research & Development Foundation
Suite 1912 - I Rockefeller Plaza
New York, New York
10020
Phone: 212—765-0750

Firms which carry large size clothing

Lane Bryant
Dept. A76–001–6
Indianapolis, Indiana
46201

Hayes
Dept. B76–001–7
Indianapolis, Indiana
46201

Lane Bryant Tall Girls
Dept. C76–001–8
Indianapolis, Indiana
46201

Roaman's
Dept. W–2
Saddle Brook, New Jersey
07662

Lana Lobell
Dept. M–2170
Hanover, Pennsylvania
17331

New Process Company
Dept. W–2
Warren, Pennsylvania
16366

Sears Roebuck & Co.
Public Relations Dept. W–2
1622 Broadway
New York, New York 10019

269

J. C. Penny
Dept. WD-2
Catalog Division
11800 West Burleigh Street
Milwaukee, Wisconsin
53263

Brownstone Studio, Inc.
Dept. W-2
342 Madison Avenue
New York, New York
10017

Old Pueblo Traders
600 South Country Club Road
W2C
Tucson, Arizona
85716

The Talbots
Dept. UK
Hingham, Massachusetts
02043

Caroll Reed
Dept. 695
North Conway, New Hampshire
03860

Johnny Appleseed's
Dept. W-2
Box 780
Dodge Street
Beverly, Massachusetts
01915

Daniel Low's
Dept. W-2
231 Essex Street
Salem, Massachusetts
01970

The Tog Shop
Dept. W-2
Lester Square
Americus, Georgia
31709

Firms which carry special-size shoes

Hill Brothers
Dept. W-2
241 Crescent Street
Waltham, Massachusetts
02154

Mooney and Gilbert
Dept. W-2
31 West 57th Street
New York, New York
10019

Shoecraft
Dept. W-2
603 Fifth Avenue
New York, New York 10017

Syd Kushner
Dept. W-2
1204 Arch Street
Philadelphia, Pennsylvania
19107

Naturalizer Shoes
Dept. W-2
21 South LaGrange Road
LaGrange, Illinois 60525

Softwear Shoes
Dept. W-2
1711 Main
Houston, Texas

Metric conversion tables

Available fabric widths

65 cm	25"
70 cm	27"
90 cm	35"/36"
100 cm	39"
115 cm	44"/45"
122 cm	48"
127 cm	50"
140 cm	54"/56"
150 cm	58"/60"
175 cm	68"/70"
180 cm	72"

Available zipper lengths

10 cm	4"
12 cm	5"
15 cm	6"
18 cm	7"
20 cm	8"
22 cm	9"
25 cm	10"
30 cm	12"
35 cm	14"
40 cm	16"
45 cm	18"
50 cm	20"
55 cm	22"
60 cm	24"
65 cm	26"
70 cm	28"
75 cm	30"

Meters to Yards

Meters	Yards
0.20	¼
0.40	½
0.60	⅝
0.80	⅞
1.00	1⅛
1.20	1⅜
1.40	1½
1.60	1¾
1.80	2
2.00	2⅛
2.20	2⅜
2.40	2⅝
2.60	2⅞
2.80	3
3.00	3¼
3.20	3½
3.40	3¾
3.60	4
3.80	4⅛
4.00	4⅜
4.20	4½
4.40	4¾
4.60	5
4.80	5⅛
5.00	5⅜

Centimeters to inches

cm	in	cm	in	cm	in
0.3	⅛	33.0	13	78.0	30¾
0.6	¼	34.0	13⅜	79.0	31⅛
1.0	⅜	35.0	13¾	80.0	31½
1.3	½	36.0	14⅛	81.0	31⅞
1.6	⅝	37.0	14⅝	82.0	32¼
1.8	¾	38.0	15	83.0	32⅝
2.0	⅞	39.0	15⅜	84.0	33⅛
2.5	1	40.0	15¾	85.0	33½
3.0	1¼	41.0	16⅛	86.0	33⅞
3.5	1½	42.0	16½	87.0	34¼
4.0	1⅝	43.0	17	88.0	34⅝
4.5	1⅞	44.0	17⅜	89.0	35
5.0	2	45.0	17¾	90.0	35⅜
5.5	2¼	46.0	18⅛	91.0	35¾
6.0	2⅜	47.0	18½	92.0	36¼
6.5	2½	48.0	18⅞	93.0	36⅝
7.0	2¾	49.0	19¼	94.0	37
7.5	3	50.0	19⅝	95.0	37⅜
8.0	3⅛	51.0	20⅛	96.0	37¾
8.5	3⅜	52.0	20½	97.0	38¼
9.0	3½	53.0	20⅞	98.0	38⅝
9.5	3¾	54.0	21¼	99.0	39
10.0	4	55.0	21⅝	100.0	39⅜
11.0	4⅜	56.0	22		
12.0	4¾	57.0	22⅜		
13.0	5⅛	58.0	22¾		
14.0	5½	59.0	23¼		
15.0	6	60.0	23⅝		
16.0	6¼	61.0	24		
17.0	6⅝	62.0	24⅜		
18.0	7	63.0	24¾		
19.0	7½	64.0	25¼		
20.0	7⅞	65.0	25⅝		
21.0	8¼	66.0	26		
22.0	8⅝	67.0	26⅜		
23.0	9	68.0	26¾		
24.0	9½	69.0	27¼		
25.0	9⅞	70.0	27⅝		
26.0	10¼	71.0	28		
27.0	10⅝	72.0	28⅜		
28.0	11	73.0	28¾		
29.0	11½	74.0	29⅛		
30.0	11¾	75.0	29½		
31.0	12¼	76.0	29⅞		
32.0	12⅝	77.0	30⅜		